SOLDIER
DOGS

SOLDIER DOGS

★ ★ ★ THE UNTOLD STORY OF ★ ★ ★
AMERICA'S CANINE HEROES

MARIA GOODAVAGE

DUTTON

DUTTON
Published by Penguin Group (USA) Inc.
375 Hudson Street, New York, New York 10014, U.S.A.
Penguin Group (Canada), 90 Eglinton Avenue East, Suite 700, Toronto,
Ontario M4P 2Y3, Canada (a division of Pearson Penguin Canada Inc.); Penguin
Books Ltd, 80 Strand, London WC2R 0RL, England; Penguin Ireland, 25 St Stephen's
Green, Dublin 2, Ireland (a division of Penguin Books Ltd); Penguin Group (Australia),
250 Camberwell Road, Camberwell, Victoria 3124, Australia (a division of Pearson
Australia Group Pty Ltd); Penguin Books India Pvt Ltd, 11 Community Centre,
Panchsheel Park, New Delhi–110 017, India; Penguin Group (NZ), 67 Apollo Drive,
Rosedale, Auckland 0632, New Zealand (a division of Pearson New Zealand Ltd);
Penguin Books (South Africa) (Pty) Ltd, 24 Sturdee Avenue, Rosebank,
Johannesburg 2196, South Africa

Penguin Books Ltd, Registered Offices: 80 Strand, London WC2R 0RL, England

Published by Dutton, a member of Penguin Group (USA) Inc.

First printing, March 2012
10   9   8   7   6   5   4   3   2

 REGISTERED TRADEMARK—MARCA REGISTRADA

LIBRARY OF CONGRESS CATALOGING-IN-PUBLICATION DATA

Goodavage, Maria, 1962–
  Soldier dogs : the untold story of America's canine heroes / Maria Goodavage.
    p. cm.
  Includes bibliographical references.
  ISBN 978-0-525-95278-7
  1. Dogs—War use—United States.   2. Dogs—Training.   3. Dogs—War use—
History.   I. Title.
  UH100.G66 2012
  355.4'24—dc23

                                                                    2011049674

Printed in the United States of America
Set in Granjon
Designed by Jaime Putorti

While the author has made every effort to provide accurate telephone numbers and
Internet addresses at the time of publication, neither the publisher nor the author
assumes any responsibility for errors, or for changes that occur after publication.
Further, the publisher does not have any control over and does not assume any
responsibility for author or third- party Web sites or their content.

★ ★ ★ CONTENTS ★ ★ ★

CONTENTS

PART FOUR
DOGS AND THEIR SOLDIERS

"Military working dogs are amazing in every aspect, and even more so when you realize that they risk their lives and save yours, all so they can have a ball."
—AIR FORCE STAFF SERGEANT
CHRISTINE CAMPOS, DOG HANDLER

PART ONE

★ ★ ★

DOGS IN HARM'S WAY

★ ★ ★ **1** ★ ★ ★

WALKING POINT

I t's 7 A.M., just north of the town of Safar, Afghanistan, and Fenji M675 is already panting. Her thick, black German shepherd coat glistens in the hot August sun. Fenji is out in front of ten marines, leashed to a D-ring that's attached to the body armor of her handler, Corporal Max Donahue. He's six feet behind her and holds his rifle ready.

Fenji leads the marines down the flat dirt road, past the trees and lush vegetation in this oasis amid the deserts of southern Afghanistan. She ignores the usual temptations: a pile of dung, a wrapper from a candy bar. Her mission doesn't include these perks. Her nose is what may keep them all alive today, and she can't distract it with the trivial. Coalition forces have been sweeping Safar of insurgents and their bombs, allowing the Safar Bazaar marketplace to reopen and locals to start living normally again. The Taliban had to go somewhere else. So they headed north. And they planted improvised explosive devices (IEDs) like seedlings among the poppy fields and grape fields and off to the sides of roads, under thick weeds.

Around here, any step you take could be your last.

And that's why Fenji is in the lead, walking point. IEDs are the top killer in Afghanistan—even with the highest technology, the best mine-sweeping devices, the most sophisticated bomb-jamming equipment, and the study of "pattern of life" activities being observed from remote piloted aircraft. But there is one response that the Taliban has no answer for: the soldier dog, with his most basic sense—smell—and his deepest desire—some praise, and a toy to chew.

"Seek!" Donahue tells Fenji, and they continue down the road, leading the men from the 3/1 (Third Battalion First Marines). She walks with a bounce to her step, tail up and bobbing gently as she half trots down the road. Every so often she stops and sniffs a spot of interest and, when she doesn't find what she's seeking, moves on. She almost looks like a dog out on a morning stroll in a park. Donahue, in full combat gear—some eighty pounds of it, including water for his dog—keeps up with her.

Fenji stops at a spot just a foot off the side of the road. She's found something of great interest. Without taking her eyes off the spot, she sniffs around it swiftly and her tail starts to wag. Suddenly she goes from standing up to lying down, staring the entire time at the spot. The men have stopped walking and are watching her. Her wagging tail kicks up some dust. Everything is silent now. No more sniffing, no crunching of boots.

Suddenly a hushed, enthusiastic voice cuts through the dead quiet. "Fenjiii! *That's* my girl!" In training exercises, Donahue is a lot more effusive, but out of respect for the bomb, he makes his initial praise short and quick, calls her back, and they "un-ass" from the area. It could be the kind of IED someone sets off from a distance, not the type that goes off when you step on it. One of the marines marks it with a chartreuse glow stick, and they move on.

Within the next hour, Fenji alerts to three more roadside bombs. Donahue lavishes her with quiet praise every time. Twice after her finds, shortly after they get away from the bombs, he tosses a black Kong toy to his dog and she easily catches it. She stands there chewing it, reveling in the sound of Donahue's praise, the feel of the hard rubber between her teeth, and the gloved hand of her best pal stroking her head. Life doesn't get much better than this for a military working dog. These are the moments these dogs live for, when all the years of training, all the hard work, come together.

"I'm proud of you!" Donahue tells her, and he means it, and she wags hard. She knows she's done well. She's been with him for seven months now, and she has a great fondness for Donahue, her first handler, and he dotes on "my sweet girl." She liked him from the moment they met at Camp Pendleton back in February. Nearly everyone who meets Donahue reacts the same way. There's something about his big personality, his love of life, his dry humor, the way he looks after you. Fenji fell right in with him, and he immediately took to her. She was young, bright, eager to learn from him, and he swears she has a sense of humor. He once said that she gets his jokes before his friends do. That's probably because she tends to wag in his presence regardless of jokes. She's just happy to be near him. She's three years old, he's twenty-three, and together they're a formidable bomb-finding force.

Their bond might contribute to their success on missions. She sleeps at the foot of Donahue's cot every night out here; she joins him for card games with the other marines; she eats next to him at the patrol base where they've been stationed during this mission. He lets her have some of his food "because my girl deserves it."

The explosive ordnance disposal (EOD) technicians usually accompany the squad but had been called to another spot this morning. They're on their way back to investigate the IEDs and defuse them. Donahue and the other marines go into action to protect the EOD techs in case of an ambush. They take positions to secure the area.

Donahue finds a great spot for his sector of fire, at a Y in the road. It's wide open here, and he can see a few hundred meters around him. He fills Fenji's portable bowl with water from his CamelBak. As she laps it up, he lies belly down, propped up on his elbows, and positions his rifle. He's facing away from the field where some of the other marines are. He's got a tiny village about two hundred meters away in his sights. If there's trouble, that's where it could start. A quenched Fenji lies down beside him a few feet away, and they wait.

The EOD techs arrive and get to work, carefully digging up the first IED, about one hundred meters from Donahue. One wrong move and they're done for, and the Taliban adds another tally mark to its scorecard. One of the techs extracts the bomb from its hiding place and bends over it to take a look. Down the road, Donahue adjusts himself slightly to get more comfortable.

Three klicks south, in Safar, Corporal Andrei Idriceanu hears a terrible explosion as he and his dog sweep a building for explosives. "That could not be good," he thinks, but he tries not to think about it too much.

★ ★ ★ **2** ★ ★ ★

REGULAR, EVERYDAY HEROES

Cairo, reportedly a Belgian Malinois, was part of the SEAL Team Six raid that led to the demise of Osama bin Laden. You don't have to be a dog lover to be fascinated by the idea that a dog—the cousin of that furry guy begging for scraps under your table—could be one of the heroes who helped execute the most vital and high-tech military mission of the new millennium.

As the first details about the operation emerged, it sometimes seemed as though the dog was more the star of the story than the Al Qaeda leader: "Enough with the discussion of the photos of Osama's corpse," rallied a blog on the Web site Gothamist, "we want to see photos of the war dog who helped take him out!"

Though the United States Naval Special Warfare Development Group (known as DEVGRU, the more recent name for SEAL Team Six) and the Department of Defense were tight-lipped about the dog's involvement in the raid, the stories poured forth. Most were conjecture presented as fact. According to some accounts, the dog sported night-vision goggles, bullet-resistant body armor, a live-action camera between his shoulders, earbuds to hear whispered commands, and rappelling gear. Not to mention four deadly titanium teeth. Holy canine superhero! Cairo's image made Batman look like a gadget-impoverished Spartan.

Night-vision goggles for an animal who already sees pretty well at night? Fake teeth? Titanium teeth are never preferable to healthy, unbroken dog teeth. They are sometimes used to replace teeth that get broken, as patrol dog teeth sometimes do. But no self-respecting veterinarian would ever yank a dog's teeth to replace them with titanium for no reason, regardless of how durable the metal is.

Concerned that some of this gear might be at least slightly exaggerated, I tried to find out the truth about Cairo, or any of his elite Special Operations multipurpose canine (MPC) brethren working dramatic missions. How hard could that be? They're just dogs, after all. We aren't talking about the Manhattan Project.

While I was visiting Joint Expeditionary Base, Little Creek, near Norfolk, Virginia, my escort pointed at the obstacle course used by the SEALs and showed me the beach where they swim. "They don't talk to *anyone* about this stuff," he told me.

These Special Ops dogs are so secret that they aren't there at all—at least some of the time. A former veterinary technician at Lackland Air Force Base in San Antonio, Texas, discovered this a couple of years ago when an Army Special Forces dog came in for treatment of some ailment. The staff treated the dog without doing the usual paperwork, and when the tech asked about some forms that were supposed to be filled out, the dog's handler told her, "This dog was never here." "From his tone, it was pretty clear. I never questioned it," she told me. "The dog didn't exist."

Oh well, never mind.

There are real canine heroes—the ones walking point, leading soldiers, sailors, airmen, and marines safely through some of the most dangerous parts of the world every day—who definitely do exist, do their jobs in harm's way without fanfare, and expect in return only a bit of praise, a chonk on a ball. They may not jump out of airplanes or fast-rope from helicopters or be rumored to have titanium teeth, but as I've come to find, the jobs they do save real lives and play an increasingly crucial role in real battlefield situations.

Throughout history, dogs have been used for attacking (disemboweling the opposition was once a favorite technique), protection, and sentry duty—alerting soldiers to danger well before they could sense it themselves. They've been trackers, messengers, sled pullers, and first-aid deliverers. As scouts, they've excelled at sniffing the air and alerting their handlers to snipers and other hidden enemies. But there may be no other time in history when their olfactory abilities have been so essential.

"My life is in my dog's nose," many handlers have told me.

In Afghanistan, where IEDs are the biggest killer, a dog's most important sense is being used more than ever: The most common job of today's military working dog (MWD) is sniffing out explosives. A trained dog can detect and alert to dozens of explosives scents. No mechanical sensor can even come close. CIA director David Petraeus praised their service when he was a four-star general: "The capability they bring to the fight cannot be replicated by man or machine."

Air Force Master Sergeant Antonio "Arod" Rodriguez, who's in charge of advising more than one hundred military working dog teams assigned to twelve air force bases, puts it this way: "The working dog is a weapons system that is resilient, compact, easily deployable, and can move fast when needed. Nothing compares."

That's part of the reason dog teams are targets. Not only do these dogs help save lives, but the information that's gathered from their finds can lead—via a very long and involved path—to locating the bigger operatives behind a device. It's not something the Taliban relishes.

Most of the traditional soldier dogs serving in Afghanistan are patrol and explosives detection dogs like Fenji. The "patrol" part means they're tough when they need to be and can put the bite on someone. I witnessed this rather personally during my research. Most patrol and explosives detection dogs in Afghanistan rarely if ever have to actively use their patrol skills, but their explosives-sniffing abilities are constantly in demand.

The lives they're saving are not just those of the troops; IEDs are not choosy about their victims. Children, families, the elderly— no one is immune to their disfiguring, deadly effects. Locals in IED-infested areas are often prisoners in their own small, mud-walled homes. Venturing outside to meet with a neighbor or get some food is fraught with danger. Whole villages have stopped functioning because no one dares to go anywhere.

There's a news video online that really brings the tragedy of the situation home for me. It shows a seven-year-old girl in Safar being rushed on a stretcher to a waiting military helicopter. She had been playing outside with her younger brother when someone stepped in the wrong place. The brother had not yet been found. His body was probably recovered later, far from the blast.

Dogs help normalize life where it has been overshadowed by constant threat of Taliban violence. These everyday paws-on-the-ground heroes and their human partners help clear villages and towns of dozens, sometimes hundreds, of explosive devices. Safar, for instance, had become a ghost town. People would not venture out. The once-thriving Safar Bazaar marketplace had been shut for months; there were so many IEDs that someone would be injured or killed there nearly every day. With all the people virtually trapped in their homes, commerce almost entirely ceased.

The dog teams came in and changed all that. In an operation that took several weeks, the village was cleared, the market declared safe. "It gives me goose bumps to think about the change. It went from dead to alive," says Corporal Idriceanu, who spent weeks helping clear the Safar Bazaar with his dog. "People could live again. I'm honored my dog and I could be part of that."

It is hard to quantify how many lives deployed soldier dog teams save by way of their detection skills. Figures range from 150 to 1,800 lives per dog. A dog who finds a bomb just as a squad is about to pass by could save several lives, depending on the bomb's strength. Maybe there would have been no lives lost, just a slight injury. Or not even that. It's impossible to count exactly how many people did not get hurt by a bomb that a dog discovered.

In any case, military working dog teams in Afghanistan were credited with finding more than 12,500 pounds of explosives in 2010. The number is probably at least slightly higher, officials say, since dogs are not always given credit for finds. Still, when you think of the damage even ten pounds of explosives in an IED can do, you can get a sense of the importance of these dogs to our military capability.

The Department of Defense has some 2,700 U.S. military working dogs in service worldwide and about six hundred serving in war zones. Another two hundred are contract dogs. Contract working dogs are trained by contractors, and their handlers work for the contractor, not the military. Most handlers in this world are former military handlers. Many got out of the military because the money is purported to be better on the contract side. Others just wanted a little more control of their jobs. If they don't want to go into a war zone, they don't have to. That's not something they could pull off when working for Uncle Sam. The Department of Defense maintains these contracts because the Military Working Dog Program can't supply enough dogs for the current need.

Even as troops start to draw down in Afghanistan, the dog teams don't show any signs of staying home for long. Because of their vital role there, many in the military dog world think the dog teams could keep deploying steadily to the end of U.S. involvement. This could put them at higher risk. Already, seventeen handlers have been killed in action since 2001, and forty-four military working dogs have died in war zones since 2005, the first year for which figures are available. (The number of dog deaths includes dogs killed in action and dogs who have died from heat injuries and other causes. The Department of Defense does not yet have a full report of causes of death.)

Military working dogs are incomparable troops, superbly well suited for their tasks. But there's something else that draws us to these dogs and their stories: For all their remarkable feats, they're not only our heroes, they're our pals. We share our homes and lives with their cousins, whose loyalty, intelligence, and unconditional love make them part of the family. When we see or read about how they're involved in war, the war becomes a little closer. It gives us a little more skin in the game. The irony is that soldier dogs make war a little more human.

UNCRATING THE HISTORY

OF WAR DOGS

W
hile I've yet to meet Cairo (or as some reports say, "Karo"), I have had the pleasure of meeting a nearly one-hundred-year-old military dog named Sergeant Stubby. The highly decorated World War I military hero died in 1926, was stuffed, and put on display at the American Red Cross Museum for nearly thirty years. His skin and hair eventually began to deteriorate, so he was taken off display. Eminent war-dog historian Michael Lemish wrote about him in his book *War Dogs: A History of Loyalty and Heroism*. He had found the dog stored in a shipping crate in an old artifacts room at the Smithsonian's National Museum of American History. The crate read: STUBBY THE DOG—FRAGILE.

While in Washington, D.C., I decided to see if I could pay homage to this granddaddy of U.S. war dogs, and I called ahead to speak with someone who knew where the old relics were stored and how I could get access. I learned that Stubby had been refurbished from nose to tail and was now once again on display. He's down the hall from Dorothy's ruby slippers, toward the end of the large exhibit called *The Price of Freedom: Americans at War*.

Stubby became a war hero at a time when the United States didn't have any semblance of a war-dog program. The small stray pit bull was taken in by a man who would make him the mascot of the 102nd Infantry in 1917. When the man went to war, he smuggled Stubby over to France by ship. Stubby provided comfort to the wounded and was devoted to his troops, but he became more than a loyal mascot. His "hero" title came to him from such feats as when he warned a sleeping sergeant of a gas attack, so that soldiers had adequate time to don their gas masks. He also bit a German infiltrator, who was hobbled by the bite and captured. The dog later suffered a shrapnel wound.

His popularity was immense, and he was grandly—if unofficially—decorated. He had to wear a blanket (given to him by several French women) to hold all his medals and pins. The dog went on to tour the United States, and he hobnobbed with three presidents.

Eighty-five years after he drew his last breath, I gazed through a glass barrier at Sergeant Stubby, who was now surrounded by a mannequin in a gas mask, an old wooden arm prosthesis, a well-preserved carrier pigeon, and other relics from the war. World War I has been relegated to a small, almost parenthetical, portion of this exhibit. Stubby looked a little plasticized, and his lip contours were bizarrely black, almost Herman Munster–ish. But this was Stubby, in the flesh, or at least in the fur.

Stubby's procurement was not a formal process, but back then in the United States, there were no rule books for war-dog procurement. In fact there was no war-dog program here at all. During World War I, European armies were using dogs to great advantage, particularly as first responders and messengers. The Red

Cross suggested a procurement process be initiated, but no appropriation was made. Someone in the General Headquarters of the American Expeditionary Forces proposed setting up a program to buy a supply of five hundred dogs every three months from the French and then setting up kennels in the United States to create a canine corps. Nothing happened.

Still, there are plenty of great stories like Stubby's, of dogs serving in combat in American units during the war, not just as mascots, but also as sentries and messengers. And certainly thousands of soldiers saw the huge benefits of using dogs in wartime. But after the war, as military budgets were drawn down, the idea of starting a war-dog program faded.

Following the attack on Pearl Harbor, the American Kennel Club and another group, Dogs for Defense, led by a prominent breeder, appealed to dog owners across the country to donate their pets to the war effort. The public response was overwhelming. And so began America's first formal military dog procurement program.

The army's logistical arm, the Quartermaster Corps, acquired thousands of dogs spanning thirty breeds during the next three years. Based in large measure on the British experience in World War I, a K-9 Corps was built around five breeds: Belgian sheepdogs, giant schnauzers, collies, German shepherds, and Doberman pinschers. In all, of about nineteen thousand dogs acquired, more than half were trained. Of those, the vast majority became sentries. As the war progressed, the need for scout dogs increased, and some 436 dogs served in the island campaigns in the Pacific.

Because so many dogs loaned during World War II proved unfit for duty—and the expense of having to return them to their owners fell to the military—the army changed its procurement policy after the war to buy its own dogs. Moreover, it set out to select dogs who could perform all the various assignments in all climates and who were bred extensively. The procurement specifications are intriguing.

He should be a sturdy compact working type, revealing evidence of power, endurance, and energy. The dog must have good bones, well-proportioned body, deep chest with ribs well sprung, strong pasterns and muscular feet with hard wall-cushioned paws. Front feet should not toe inward or outward, hind quarters should have moderate angulation, and, as viewed from the rear, hind legs should be straight. The temperament of the dog should show general alertness, steadiness, vigor and responsiveness. He should not be timid, nervous, gun or noise-shy. In addition, the dog must be from nine months to three years old, must be between 22 inches and 28 inches high at the shoulder and must weigh between 60 and 90 pounds. The dog may be either male or female, but a female must have been spayed 60 days prior to being offered for purchase.

Hard wall-cushioned paws?

One by one, breeds were discounted. Climate was one deciding factor. Dobermans worked well only in temperate climates; collies, Siberian huskies, and Alaskan malamutes in colder climates. Labs and other sporting breeds were not considered dependable because of their gaming instinct. In the end, the German shepherd became the dog of choice as the Korean War began in June 1950.

But with all the talk about how successful dogs had been in World War II and the forging of a real procurement policy, as the curtain went up on the Korean War only one dog unit went into action: the Twenty-sixth Infantry Scout Dog Platoon. It did well, and there was a plan to attach a scout dog platoon to each division, but then the war ended.

And that marked a hiatus in the military's dog program. The procurement stopped. The army war-dog program was defunded, and rumors spread that the program would be abandoned entirely. This drew an emotional, angry public response. The program survived; the air force took it over and started a training center at Lackland Air Force Base in San Antonio, Texas.

But in the late 1950s and early 1960s, as America's involvement in Vietnam intensified, and as the air force began to see the labor-saving advantages of sentry dogs, demand outstripped supply. Moreover, there was no military pipeline, or even a civilian pipeline like Dogs for Defense, to bring more dogs to the effort.

The result was that the military was forced into a hurry-up scenario, and quickly sent out small teams of recruiters to bases around the country to buy up dogs from neighboring communities. The price paid was usually not more than $150 per dog. The breeds of dogs procured once again expanded, and Labradors and even hounds were among those drafted. Some 3,800 dogs would serve during the course of this war.

War dog procurement is partly a matter of selecting breeds for combat and then drawing a steady supply, but it's also a matter of demilitarization and repatriation. That was assumed after World War II but forgotten after Vietnam, when thousands of dogs were left behind, either to replenish supplies for the South Vietnamese

Army or to be eaten, as some have asserted, or simply euthanized. Some handlers even chose to reenlist so they could be with their dogs as long as possible, in hopes they might be able to prolong the dogs' lives and perhaps even adopt them.

The situation now is utterly transformed. Our understanding of dogs' qualities and abilities is far better, and the results of our working together in the military are vastly improved. So does this new kind of military use have anything to offer back to our understanding of, or relationship with, our own dogs at home?

★ ★ ★ 4 ★ ★ ★

JAKE, THE EVERYDOG
WITH THE RIGHT STUFF?

I'd written about other military working dogs before Cairo and Sergeant Stubby. And every time I did, I found myself looking at my own dog.

In the haze of glory surrounding military working dogs, my dog Jake, who is now nine, doesn't really look like a contender for admission into the military elite. When he was younger, did he have what it took to sniff out bombs, to risk his life, to walk point in order to save others? I'd look at him, typically lying around sleeping somewhere and perhaps snoring, or absconding with an unattended bit of food, or rolling in the grass. Not obviously military hero material.

But Jake does have his breed going for him. He's a Labrador retriever—a breed the military commonly uses for detection work. Actually, we're not 100 percent sure he's all Lab. He was found wandering the streets of a seedy part of San Francisco at six months of age. A rescue group took him in and we agreed to foster him. It was to be just for a week or two. Our old Airedale had died the previous month, and we weren't ready for a dog to take up a full-time, permanent position in our house. This was to be a temp gig. But the minute he walked in the door, on December 1, 2002, I knew we were in trouble. He was all paws, with a big smile on his wide blond face, and bright brown eyes that scanned the foyer, looked at me, and gave me that "Yup, I'm home! Get used to me!" look.

Jake does show some signs of being a good potential war dog. He bonded with us quickly, he is eager to please, would do anything for us (except stop chewing flip-flops), and is pretty fearless. He's also a great sniffer. I have yet to find a place to hide his dog treats where he doesn't sit staring at the invisible wafting scent, obsessed, clearly trying to figure out ways to maneuver them down from their stealth position, and often succeeding.

But military dogs have something Jake doesn't: a job. It's something dog experts say is lacking with many pet dogs today, and is at the root of many problems. Boredom can lead to destructive or anxious behavior. At best, it's just not much fun.

"Dogs used to have jobs; that's what they were trained to do," dog trainer Victoria Stillwell, host of the Animal Planet show *It's Me or the Dog*, told me when I ran into her at an event honoring hero dogs in Los Angeles. "Now these poor animals spend most of the time sitting on the couch, alone all day. They're bored. We need to give them jobs. If they're motivated by them, if they enjoy themselves, life is better all the way around."

I started to feel bad that Jake didn't have a job, but then I realized he's like me. He's kind of a self-employed freelancer. He finds work that he's passionate about and puts everything into the job until his mission is accomplished.

His current gig is rather cliché: He lies in wait in our backyard much of the day, so he can chase a relatively new neighborhood cat,

Kika, out of the yard when she ventures over the fence. (He never gets closer than several yards from the cat, or I'd put the kibosh on it.) She's a beautiful, lithe, leopard-spotted feline, and I welcomed her into our yard until I saw her chasing and killing butterflies, and until I found out why my little writing cottage smelled like a litter box every time I opened the front window. (She was using the bit of dirt right outside my window as her toilet.)

When Jake is in the house and he hears her little bell, he races down the stairs and out to the backyard. When he runs after her, he looks more like a rocking horse, cantering merrily, tail woggling quickly from side to side and up and down. He doesn't seem to take the chase too seriously. A big woof or two and Kika is out of the yard through a hole in the lattice of the back fence. Only then can Jake rest, a job well done.

Jake is an Everydog. His is the most popular breed of dog in the United States. He's even got one of the most common names for male dogs. And his passion for chewing shoes and chasing cats and finding food are charmingly stereotypical.

He pokes around in this book. You can think of him as a stand-in for your dog or other pet dogs if you find yourself wondering, as I did and still do, how the average dog would fare in the military.

Having an Everydog in the mix puts war dogs into perspective. Military dogs may have unique breeding and intense training, but underneath it all, they're dogs. Unless they're of the super-aggressive variety, many go on to become pets at the ends of their careers. (A huge improvement from post-Vietnam days.) Inside, most probably just want to catch a ball and get a pat for a job well done, eat some good grub, and sleep in a comfortable bed near their favorite person.

Most maybe. But "some dogs are just jerks" I was told by an air force technical sergeant who has worked with every type of dog during his decade in the world of handlers. There are the dogs, for instance, who will seem to reach out to you and beckon you to pet them, but once you do, they try to bite your hand off. "They get this look in their eye like 'Heh heh heh,'" he said. "Just like people, some dogs are bad guys."

★ ★ ★ 5 ★ ★ ★

THE MEANING OF
MILITARY DOG TATTOOS

Military working dogs are considered equipment by the Department of Defense. In some ways, they're officially looked upon as a rifle or a minesweeper would be. It's a designation that fell upon military dogs after World War II, when the military stopped borrowing dogs from Mom and Pop Dog Lover and started buying dogs.

And it just so happens that dogs may be the only "equipment" that get tattoos.

Of course, handlers see their dogs as anything but equipment. Handlers put their lives on the line for their dogs, and the reverse is also true. During the Korean War, the handler of a dog named Judy was taken prisoner and forced to march for two days to his place of detention. When he got there, he unleashed Judy and begged her to run, hoping she'd make it back to HQ. But she stayed at his side. The next day Chinese guards took them to a kitchen and made him tie Judy to a post and leave her. They asked him who Judy was, and he told them she was a mascot.

"I heard a gunshot. I am sure it was Judy," he wrote.

When soldier dogs and handlers deploy, they spend almost every hour together. Like Donahue and Fenji, they rarely leave each other's side when they're at war. Handlers can end up developing a closer bond with their dogs than they do with other people, even spouses. When a handler and his dog have to part from each other in order to fulfill a unit requirement, it can be enough to bring the handler to tears, and to cause a dog to ignore his new handler—at least for awhile.

I've never seen anyone cry when she talks about turning in her old rifle or giving back her body armor. The fact that dogs are still considered equipment seems rather antiquated. Sure, they're not human soldiers, but they're a far cry from a rifle or a helmet or a helicopter. Ask any child who watches *Sesame Street* which of these things does not belong, and the tot will point right to the dog. Most instructors and trainers will, too.

"I try to articulate that a dog is *not* a piece of equipment, but a working, breathing animal that needs to be treated respectfully and kindly," says Arod, who also runs Olive Branch K-9, a police and military dog consultancy. "Your dog is your partner and values meaningful interaction. You just don't think about equipment in the same way."

Some handlers I've spoken with hope that at some point four-legged warriors will be given a new designation. Even something like "animal personnel" would be more accurate than "equipment" and would take dogs out of the "thing" category. Dogs could be joined in that category by other animals used by the military, like the sea lions, dolphins, and whales used by Navy SEALs to find sea mines and enemy divers.

★

In this book, you'll notice that in most cases where I mention a dog's name for the first time, it's followed by a letter and three numerals. That's a dog's tattoo number, his unique ID, inked inside his left ear. If you view a dog as equipment, it could be like his VIN. If you see a dog as something more, think of it as his last name.

Here's a way to use a dog's tattoo number to win a bar bet with a handler. You can tell a handler what year his dog arrived at Lackland Air Force Base—where young future military working dogs go for processing and training—just by knowing the first letter of the tattoo. Even most handlers I spoke with weren't sure how their dogs came by their tattoo numbers. But it's fairly simple.

Tattoos start with a new letter every year. The year 2011, when I arrived at Lackland Air Force Base, was an R year.

So let's say you come upon Handler Joe and his dog Bella M430. Tell him you can guess pretty close to when his dog arrived at Lackland for the first time. Then all you have to do is figure out how many letters earlier than the current year's letter M is. If you'd met Joe and Bella M430 in 2011, during the R year, you'd calculate the numerical difference between M and R. So M-N-O-P-Q-R—that's six letters. But don't blurt out that Joe's dog arrived five years ago. The letters G, I, O, Q, and U are not used in tattoos because they can easily be confused for other letters or numbers. So in the case of Bella M430, you "add back" two years (for O and Q) and now you can safely say that Bella arrived at Lackland for processing three years ago. Since most dogs get to Lackland when they're two or three, you could take it a step further and figure that Bella is five or six years old.

Beers all around!

I'm not sure how much Sergeant Stubby had to do with this, but a military myth holds that a dog is always one rank above his handler. The popularity of this story spiked after the bin Laden raid.

The truth is that, officially, dogs hold no rank—equipment never does. (Equipment doesn't let you bury your face in its fur when you're mourning a fallen comrade, either.) It would also be confusing when a dog gets transferred between handlers of different ranks. There would be a lot of demotions and promotions in a dog's career—not that the dog would care.

That's not to say that some handlers don't refer to their dogs as the next rank up. I've never come across a marine handler who did this, but it's a fairly strong tradition in the army, where it probably started during World War II. Some say it was a move to get handlers not to abuse their dogs, because they could be in trouble for abusing a superior. Others believe it was just a maneuver to warm the hearts of Americans so they'd support the war-dog program and donate their dogs to the fight.

Even in army ceremonies honoring a dog for his service, the dog will often be referred to by his rank. And handlers have fun with it in everyday life, too.

"On occasion we tease lower-ranking soldiers if they ask to pet our working dogs," says Army Sergeant Amanda Ingraham. "We tell them if they do pet our dogs, they need to do so at the position of parade rest and show our NCO some respect. It's all in fun, but at the same time it gets everyone to realize the value of our dogs."

And non-handlers will also notice the names of dogs tattooed on their fellow servicemen's arms or legs.

Ink all around!

★ ★ ★ 6 ★ ★ ★

HEY, IS THAT 600 ROUNDS OF
ANTIAIRCRAFT AMMUNITION?

Early in the research for this book, I got a note from Brandon Liebert, a former marine sergeant who had been a handler and trainer for eight years. He deployed to Iraq in 2004 with one of the first groups of garrison handlers sent into a war zone. He's now a civilian contractor, working as a dog handler. He gave me one of my first insights into who dog handlers are.

Dear Maria,

During my time at MCAS Cherry Point, NC (March 2003– August 2006), I only handled one dog. His name is Monty E030, a Patrol Explosive Detector Dog. He and I had a great bond. He was a very fast learner and loved to please me. Because I trained him to do more than what the military required, I ended up making sure he had a different toy for every task. He also had his personal toys. He had more toys than any other dog in the kennels. Every morning we would go out and play before starting any type of training. Even though we were not supposed to, I would feed him some human food while we would be out on patrols. While deployed to Iraq, I would take Monty with me everywhere (i.e., chow hall, internet cafe, phone center, etc). Taking him with me everywhere also helped in keeping up the morale of the troops. They loved to play with him, pet him, help me with his training. Having him around all the time was not only fun and good times for me but also the troops, whether it was on base or out in the field.

When we were in Iraq, we celebrated the Marine Corps Birthday. The Marine Corps flew in steaks for us. I asked the cooks if they would save a leftover one for me so I could give it to Monty, and they did. So we both had steak for the Marine Corps Birthday. He sure did love it.

I would do anything for him and he would do anything for me. I had full confidence in him when he alerted to something. If he was not confident about something, I could tell. He could read me and I could read him. That is how good our bond was. When I had to give him up to another handler and change duty stations, it was hard. I felt like I had lost my best friend. We had bonded for over 3 years and now it was time to say goodbye. It was harder for me to say goodbye to him than what it was to say goodbye to everyone in the kennels. But he had a new daddy, so I had to move on.

It was an intriguing note to get at the start of this project. Here was a marine who referred to himself as the dog's "daddy," a warrior who felt a lump in his throat when parting with his best friend of three years. His tender ways with his dog clashed with the image I'd always had of marines as super-tough, aggressive combatants.

I wondered: Was Liebert the exception, or was he typical of military dog handlers?

As I came to see, Liebert's closeness with his dog was not unusual. Phrases like "He'd do whatever it took to save my life, and I'd do the same to save his," or "She was like my child," come up all the time when talking to handlers. The stories handlers told me made it clear that the closer a handler feels to her dog, the better the working relationship tends to be. In the end, that translates into saved lives. If a handler knows a dog well, she's going to know what subtle signs to watch when the dog is looking for explosives or bad guys.

I met up with Liebert and his fiancée, Amanda Lothian, when they were passing through San Francisco. No longer obligated to uphold marine standards, he wore his dark hair slicked back in a tidy ponytail and sported a trim beard and mustache. He'd met Lothian at Lackland Air Force Base, where she was a vet tech. She left the army for civilian work shortly before having their baby. She went into labor as Liebert was getting on a plane to go train as a dog handler. "I'm sorry," he told her on the phone when she— in the throes of contractions—called him. "I have to get to the dogs."

Dogs are still front and center in their lives. When we met at the rooftop bar at the Marines Memorial Hotel, Liebert was awaiting a high-security clearance for his second round of contract work in Afghanistan. He is now "daddy" to a German shepherd mutt, Mabel. When stateside, he plans vacations around her, refusing to put her on a plane, and taking her in his truck on road trips instead. The dog will be staying with his sister while he's away for the next year. Lothian is now a vet tech at the Veterinary Medical Teaching

Hospital at the University of California, Davis, and has a German shepherd, Archimedes.

Liebert and Lothian both sport tattoos of dog paws on their lower legs. His paw tattoo is big and burly and is flanked by the words "Dogs of War." Hers is a replica of her dog's paw, with the name written in dainty italics underneath.

With introductions made, drinks in hand, and the pianist gliding his way through the entire song list from *Phantom of the Opera*, Liebert begins to recount the story of his dog Monty's greatest day, his biggest find in Iraq. Liebert's voice sounds remarkably like Jimmy Stewart's when the actor was young. I'll let him tell it.

"We were in a little forward operating base (FOB) in a town called Husayba. The commander of the base was given information about threats made to the Iraqi Civil Defense Corps (ICDC) unit there. These threats came from a group of insurgents looking to take over the ICDC compound. They feared the worst, so the unit chose to abandon their compound, which was located just a few hundred yards away from our base. If the insurgents were to take over this building, it would give them a good advantage to try and take over our base.

"We got to the building with no resistance and had to sweep it for explosives. When we started searching inside, Monty led me to a back room. On the way he alerted to a mortar round and an anti-tank mine that had been taken apart. We continued toward the back room again, and when we walked in, he started to circle the room. This usually means that there's a high concentration of odor and he can't pinpoint where exactly the odor is coming from. The only things in the room were these huge metal boxes. I brought him over to them so he could search them, and he gave me a final response. Something was there.

"One of the boxes was slightly open, so I looked inside as much as I could without touching it. From what I could see, there were bullet rounds in it. I notified the sergeant in charge and we had a couple of marines guard that area while I continued. In the next room, we found the weapon for those rounds. It was some type of antiaircraft gun with a swivel mounting system. Eventually we went over to a medium-size building with only one room. Monty alerted to an area against the inside wall where there was a mound of dirt and some trash. We secured the area and had the EOD team come out and check the areas where Monty had responded.

"According to EOD, Monty found over six hundred antiaircraft rounds and a 155mm round. It was the biggest find our K-9 group had while we were there. I was so proud of him, and he was really happy, because he knew he did a great job. He loved to work for his toy, and he loved to work for me, so it was really all just big fun for him."

I ask him what could have happened if Monty had not found those rounds. "If those rounds had been used," he says, pausing and taking a long draw on his drink, "you just don't want to think about what they can do with those things."

We talk more about their adventures together. About how the dog cheered up troops by his mere presence. About the array of different toys Liebert gave Monty for successfully completing tasks. "If you were given a steak dinner every time you did something good, it would get old after a while."

Eventually we come to how Liebert and Monty had to part

ways. The pianist is playing "Don't Cry for Me Argentina" now. Another round of drinks comes our way.

When they came back from Iraq, they had more time together at the kennels for several months until Monty was assigned to another handler who would be deploying to Iraq with him two months later. Liebert likened it to having your child assigned to another parent. "It's disconcerting, really hard, especially when you've been together as long as we had." But he knew this came with the territory of being a military dog handler, and he steeled himself.

He wasn't supposed to interact much with Monty at that point, because the new handler needed to build up a rapport with him. So Liebert would pet him through the fence. Every once in a while he'd get in the kennel with him and hold on to him and hug him. "I told him, 'Hey, I'm your stepdaddy now, that's your new daddy.'"

The handler and Monty deployed, did their tour, and came back safely. Not too long after they got back, Monty was put up for adoption for a medical reason Liebert wasn't privy to. He handed in his adoption packet immediately, but he learned that Monty had already been adopted out, probably to another handler. He's not sure who got Monty, because there was an incident toward the end that caused a rift between him and the people who made the decision in the kennel. He doesn't go into it. He kept busy, spending the next four years, from 2006 to 2010, as a dog trainer at Lackland Air Force Base. He left in mid-2010 in order to make more money as a dog handler in the private sector.

He had several good months as a contract dog handler in Afghanistan, working with Loebes, a black shepherd, but he can't imagine anyone will ever take Monty's place. Some days he wonders if Monty, who would be a senior citizen by now, is still around. "All I can do is hope and pray that whoever has him is taking care of him and giving him the life that he deserves as a retired military working dog."

7

THIS IS THE LIFE

Ask almost any handler how he likes the work, and you'll hear something like this: "It's the best job in the world." I've never heard this phrase so much as I did while exploring the world of military working dogs. These are people who go to hellish areas and get shot at and risk their lives every day, and they say things like "I wouldn't trade working with my dog for anything," or "Canine is a lot of hard work, a lot of extra hours, but, I mean, it's a *dog*."

These men and women (women make up only 10 percent of handlers) don't all come from a dog background, but those who make it through the intensive training and end up with a canine partner are passionate about what they do. Handlers tend to be type A personalities who, by their own admission, often get along better with dogs than people. Not that they don't like people. It's just that they get to know dogs so well. Handlers in war zones must rely on the dogs for their very lives. Along the way they get to know the hearts and souls of their dogs. "It's better than with people," one handler told me. "It's just simpler, and more pure."

A big fear some handlers have is that their home kennel won't get enough dogs, and they'll become just regular MPs, which is where most started out. Once you've worked with these dogs, once you've experienced that bond, it seems the idea of becoming a regular "straight legs" is a lonely proposition.

Army Corporal Kory Wiens called his mine-detection dog, a Labrador retriever named Cooper, "my son." He bought him all kinds of toys, and they sometimes shared a cot while on deployment in Iraq.

Wiens, twenty, planned to reenlist so he could stay with Cooper and adopt him when the dog was at the end of his career. He would never get that chance. Wiens and his dog were killed by an IED while on patrol in Muhammad Sath in July 2007.

His family knew how important Cooper was to Wiens. The pair's cremated remains are buried together in a cemetery in Wiens's hometown of Dallas, Oregon.

8

THE KILLING FIELDS, WITH DOG

W hat was bad in Iraq is worse in Afghanistan.

The first handler I reached in Afghanistan was an army staff sergeant named Marcus Bates. In an e-mail, he introduced himself with characteristic military formality. "My name is SSG Bates, Marcus, serving in the U.S. Army," he began. Bates wanted to talk about his partner, Davy N532, a three-year-old Belgian Malinois, whose name didn't match her gender.

Bates recounted how he and Davy were supporting the Fourth Battalion Twenty-fifth Field Artillery Regiment, in Kandahar Province. During their months together they'd already found 140 pounds of explosives, two grenades, and two mortars.

"We get action about every time we go on a mission," Bates said. He described Davy as a top-notch patrol and explosives detection dog. She'd been with Bates for nineteen months, at home base and in theater. "I trust her with my life. If I didn't trust her, I wouldn't be here."

Bates had deployed with a dog once before, in Iraq. But Davy is new to war. In fact, Bates is her first handler. They hit it off immediately and she sleeps on his cot. She starts off with her head on his chest, but by the morning she is sleeping nestled up to his feet.

She's slight for her breed, weighing only forty-five pounds, but her size turns out to be an asset in more than just sleeping arrangements. She's agile enough to scramble up and over the four- to five-foot-high hardened mud walls that surround the area's notorious grape fields. When Bates thinks of other handlers having to hoist eighty-pound German shepherds over those walls, he's grateful for Davy. His combat load is already fifty to sixty pounds, including weapons, ammo, and enough water and food to last both of them for a two-day mission.

One November day Bates and Davy were on patrol in a grape field when they came under fire from eighty yards away. "I hate the grape fields here."

Grape fields in Afghanistan are a far cry from your standard lush, manicured Western vineyards. Grapes grow in sprawling, tangled rows, between humid, muddy ditches obscured by weeds. The trenches are notoriously good places to hide explosives. When a blast goes off, the narrowness of the trench concealing it intensifies the explosion. These are the killing fields of a new generation of soldier.

As bullets from the AKs flew past, Bates and his squad took cover and returned fire. After a while it was time to get away from the dangerous trenches and up close with the enemy. The squad leader and Bates, Davy alongside, moved swiftly toward the enemy, firing as they approached.

The insurgents bolted and disappeared. But their secret ally—in the form of a long strand of copper wire in the dirt—remained.

Bates and his little team followed the wire to a nearby grape hut. It was a small mud barn with thick walls pocked with holes for hanging fruit, as well as opium and marijuana, depending on the season. They entered, with Davy's nose leading the way. Bates followed the wire to a battery. It was the makings of a command-wire IED. All someone had to do was touch the battery to the wire, and an IED on the other end would explode "on command." When Bates looked up, Davy was sitting down staring at a pile of branches. She sat there, head tilted slightly down, riveted to the branches as if lost in a good book.

"My first thought was 'Holy crap what is right next to me?'"

Bates approached the pile gingerly and found a vest with two grenades and some intel on local insurgents. A short time later, Davy discovered two IEDs near the hut.

It is clear that the bond between handlers and dogs on the battlefield is extraordinarily powerful. But wait. Before we go any further, there is a question we must address. Is it right to use dogs in war? Should we be putting them in harm's way at all? Why should dogs die for the arguments of men? After all, dogs don't have any say in the matter. They're drafted and serve faithfully. They probably don't understand the concept of death. This is all a big game to them, in a way. It's about chasing a ball and bonding with a handler and having fun and getting praised.

I don't have a complete, perfect answer to this question. I love dogs. The first time I met a military working dog, I wanted to abscond with him. He seemed happy at his home station of Travis

Air Force Base, near Fairfield, California. But I found out he was going to war the next month. He had no worries about this, of course, but his innocence made his fate seem almost heartbreaking. "Hey, pal," I wanted to tell him, "see that old station wagon over there? Make a break for it in one minute and I'll meet you there. Do I ever have a nice dog bed for you, and there's this dog named Jake I think you'd like."

As the months went by, I met more dogs and handlers, and learned about the lives they saved, and saw the bonds they forged. I saw that, despite the less-than-ideal work conditions, these dogs have something a lot of pampered dogs don't: a purpose, something meaningful in their lives.

It's something we all aspire to.

I came to see just how incredible the best of these dogs are. If I had to cover a war, I'd want to be in a unit loaded with soldier dogs. Ditto if I had a kid who was in the military.

But just who are these dogs? Is there something that makes them entirely different from your dog or Jake, or even that rugged German shepherd you see in the neighborhood? Is it just their training or is it something in their bloodlines? That is the question at the core of the next part of this book.

PART TWO

★ ★ ★

NATURE, NURTURE, AND TRAINING

9

SHOPPING IN EUROPE

There are no ad campaigns to entice soldier dogs to join the military, no jingles about being all the dog you can be. Dogs don't visit recruiters to weigh the options of civilian versus military life. They have no say about whether they'll spend their days as couch potatoes or canine combatants.

In the mid-1980s, the Department of Defense started looking toward Europe for dogs. Belgium, the Netherlands, Germany, and France sold the U.S. dogs who were essentially castoffs, by-products of the working-dog sports established there for seventy-five to one hundred years or more. Devoted amateurs made it their avocation to breed, rear, and train dogs in police-like work. They would sell their excess dogs to whatever agencies wanted them. This kicked in the demand for more of this kind of dog in Europe, and a market was born.

Soldier dogs are called to serve their country. But their country is unlikely to be their country of origin. If it were, these dogs would serve the military of places like Bulgaria, the Czech Republic, Slovakia, Hungary, Poland, the Netherlands, and Germany. Although some military dogs are purchased in the U.S., even the bulk of American-bought military dogs originally hail from these parts of Europe. They just happen to be brought back by vendors in the U.S. to be sold here.

The Department of Defense dog program wants to buy American to support American business, so who are these dogs who are so special they have to be imported from Europe? Are they so top-notch that we can't produce them here? And what about Jake and other average American dogs? Would they have had a stab at being war dogs? Would Jake have passed the stringent testing to become a military working dog, at least back when he was a lad?

I sorted through my questions about soldier dog procurement with Stewart Hilliard, the MWD breeding program manager, who headed dog procurement for years and is still involved in procurement evaluations. "Doc Hilliard," or "Doc," as he's known around here, is a civilian who works at Lackland Air Force Base, set in the dry, rugged terrain on the outskirts of San Antonio. The base is at the center of the military working dog universe. Let's step inside one of the new buildings here.

To enter, you have to dip the soles of your shoes in a vat of green disinfectant called Roccal-D that looks eerily like the acidic "Dip" from *Roger Rabbit*. My escort, Gerry Proctor, and I tramped upstairs with slightly damp, smelly shoes.

The "Doc" in Doc Hilliard comes from his PhD in behavioral neuroscience, which he likes to point out "is a fancy term for animal learning." With a name like Doc, one might expect a short, plump, older, bespectacled man, perhaps with a white fringe of beard. So when a six-foot-four, fit, clean-shaven, brown-haired man walked into the large meeting room, it was a bit surprising.

Doc Hilliard has worked in just about every capacity with big, strong dogs for decades. He began training working dogs in 1980 and went on to specialize in Schutzhund and other dog sports popular in Europe—sports that test dogs for traits like courage, protective instinct, intelligence, and perseverance. These are vital qualities in law-enforcement dogs and military working dogs. Doc made a name for himself in the field and eventually got plucked up by the Military Working Dog Program. He's been at Lackland since 1997 and has worked in every capacity, from dog behavior evaluator to the director of training for the program. These days, bringing the best dogs for the buck to the U.S. military is his main concern.

About five or six times a year, Doc and a small embassy of veterinarians, vet techs, handlers, and evaluators fly from San Antonio to Europe to buy young dogs they hope will become soldier dogs. During these buy trips, the team visits roughly five dog brokers in Western Europe, primarily in the Netherlands. The team's goal is to supply hundreds of new working dogs for the Department of Defense annually.

If talking about dogs in terms of brokers sounds impersonal, then the synonymous term *vendors* is even less warm and fuzzy. But, again, officially these pooches are considered equipment, not soldiers. Vendors buy dogs from breeders in order to sell them to governments and law-enforcement organizations. They develop relationships with breeders, buying hundreds of dogs a year from them, and putting them all up for one-stop shopping for military entities.

Visiting a vendor has been likened to going to a flea market, but other than having dozens or hundreds of items (dogs) in one area, there's actually little resemblance. The U.S. team isn't jostling with the military buyers from other countries. On the days Doc Hil-liard's crew goes in to buy, it's U.S. only. And there is no haggling, no "This dog is worth twice that! You should see what that guy over there from Yemen will give me for him, and don't get me started on that South African buyer!" Prices are set by strict govern-ment purchase rules and regulations. The Department of Defense publishes a requirement, and brokers compete to fulfill the require-ment with the lowest possible priced dogs for what the U.S. needs.

No one—not even Doc Hilliard—will officially say how much the dogs cost. The closest Doc will come is "You couldn't buy a new car with the money, but it's substantial." A few sources close to the buying process say when the U.S. buys in bulk, we get dual-purpose (patrol and detection) dogs for somewhere between $3,000 and $4,500. The price adds up when you consider how many dogs we buy each year, but it's far less than some other countries pay.

The Israeli Defense Forces, for instance, have a reputation for buying the strongest, most resilient dogs available and paying top dollar—upward of $7,000 per standard military dog, and occasion-ally even double that. Of course, Israel needs far fewer dogs than the U.S. does, so the country can afford to spend more on a dog. But there are plenty of handlers and trainers who wish the U.S. could spend the money needed for superior genetics in order to get dogs who have the ability to better withstand the rigors of war, from their physical robustness to their unflappable mental makeup.

"Compared to the dogs that bring top dollar, our dogs aren't really the best. The buy teams do whatever they can within the financial limits, and trainers and handlers can make a shit dog into an excellent war dog, but it would be helpful to be able to pay for a better product," I was told by a longtime MWD trainer.

Doc Hilliard isn't sure that spending more money is the answer. Training and maturity can take a dog from zero to sixty in no time. "We get a lot of first-class animals. And dogs that don't look first-class while in training may become awesome working animals in the field with maturity and experience."

More than one-tenth of the dogs the U.S. buys will end up as washouts, failing to meet the Military Working Dog Program's physical or behavioral standards. These dogs have problems that weren't evident during the lengthy testing of the dogs by the dog-buying team. Most of the troubles stem from environmental issues, like fear of loud gunfire and explosions, or the inability to learn necessary basic tasks. Like people, some dogs are just slow learners. "Some are Einsteins, some are rocks," says veterinarian Walter Burghardt, chief of behavioral medicine and military working dog studies at Lackland's Daniel E. Holland Military Working Dog Hospital. Since they have only a set amount of time to go through the canine version of basic training, the dogs who take too long to learn aren't going to make the cut.

Some of the failed dogs become "training aids"—dogs who help students at Lackland's dog-handler school learn the basics of dog handling. Dogs who aren't aggressive enough to do both patrol and explosives work can become explosives dogs only and can still deploy. Others can go to local law-enforcement agencies or can be adopted out to the public.

Ten percent isn't a bad attrition rate compared with what it was just five to six years ago, when more than one-fourth of the dogs bought by the United States would end up washing out. Improved training techniques—with more carrot, less stick—may have a lot to do with the success of these dogs, say those who have been involved with the dog program for the last decade. It makes sense. Would you rather work for someone who gets really nasty when you don't do something perfectly, or for someone who notices the good stuff and isn't usually too harsh about the less-than-stellar performances?

Better knowledge of what goes into making a strong military working dog accounts for some of the increase in dog draftees who go on to become soldier dogs. Hilliard and his team spend most of their time at the vendors running tests on the dogs, evaluating everything from general health to the desire to chase a ball, to see if dogs—even those bought on a lean budget—have what it takes.

★ ★ ★ **10** ★ ★ ★

THE DIVERSITY OF MWD JOBS

The nature and nurture of military dogs is complicated because of their breeding and where they come from, to be sure, but it is necessarily diverse because there is such a range of jobs they do. To understand which breeds of dogs get selected for which jobs in the military, it helps to know a little about the range of roles these dogs have. You might think "Seen one military working dog, seen 'em all"—but these dogs are as varied as the soldiers, sailors, airmen, and marines they work beside.

Just about everything in the military has an acronym, from the sublime (COPPER for Chemoterrorism Operations Policy for Public Emergency) to the ridiculous (POO for Point of Origin; when a dog handler told me about how he had to go back to the POO in order to start his mission, it painted an odd picture). Military working dog jobs are no exception. It is simpler to divide the dogs into some broad categories and then tap into the acronyms.

Single-purpose dogs are used for one purpose only: sniffing out explosives or narcotics (or in the case of combat tracking dogs, humans). They tend to be "sporting" breeds, like Labrador retrievers,

51

golden and Chesapeake Bay retrievers, Viszlas, and various short- and wire-haired pointers. Jack Russell terriers and even small poodles sometimes make appearances.

Single-purpose dogs don't need to be aggressive. They can be all nose, no bite. Some single-purpose dogs might get naturally protective, but as most handlers of dogs like Labs will attest, they're more likely to lick you to death. A couple of the jobs (CTDs and MDDs) tend to employ dogs more typically associated with dual-purpose work, like German shepherds, Belgian Malinois, and Dutch shepherds.

These dogs are trained to locate either drugs *or* explosives—never both. You don't want to have to stand there guessing if Balco M492 is alerting to a stash of heroin or a pressure-plate IED. "When your dog makes an alert, you need to know whether to run away and call the explosives people or whether to go arrest someone," says Doc Hilliard.

Types of single-purpose dogs and the jobs they do include:

EDD (explosive detector dog)—This is your standard-fare single-purpose dog, used in all branches of the military. The handlers of these dogs are military police who spend months going through dog-handler school at Lackland Air Force Base.

NDD (narcotics detector dog)—Just like the EDD, except this dog detects drugs instead of explosives.

SSD (specialized search dog)—This dog goes a step beyond EDD work. SSD dogs are a special class of dogs trained to work off leash at long distances from a handler in order to find explosives. They work by hand signals and in the marines can also receive commands via radio receivers they wear on their backs. (The air force and the navy don't have SSDs.) These dogs can also be breeds that are usually reserved as dual-purpose dogs, like German shepherds.

CTD (combat tracker dog)—Explosives dogs and SSDs can detect where IEDs and weapons caches are located, but it's up to the highly trained CTDs to track down the person who stashed the explosives. This is a marine program only. Although the job is in our single-purpose dog list, combat tracker dogs are more typically dual-purpose dog breeds these days. "Labs were too goofy for the work," a longtime CTD trainer told me. CTDs generally work on a long retractable leash.

MDD (mine detection dog)—These dogs do slow and steady off-leash searches for buried mines and artillery. This is an army program only. Labs, shepherds, and Malinois are the preferred breeds for this job.

TEDD (tactical explosive detector dog)—Lackland doesn't procure dogs for the army's TEDD program. Contractors do, and they generally buy them from U.S. vendors. The program is a temporary one created in response to a request from former general David Petraeus for an influx of special sniffer dogs to help with IED detection. Select infantrymen from deploying units are given short-term training on how to work with these dogs, who are trained by contractors.

IDD (IED detector dog)—As with TEDDs, this is a temporary program created to fulfill the urgent need for bomb dogs. It's run by the Marine Corps and accounts for the majority of sporting breed dogs in the Department of Defense Military Working Dog Program. The dogs are bought from breeders and vendors around the U.S. by contractors, who train them and the infantrymen who will be their handlers. (The training of IDD handlers and TEDD handlers is far shorter than that of other MWD handlers—many say too short to ensure the safest and most effective dog teams.)

Dual-purpose dogs do both patrol work (protection, aggression when needed) and detection work, along with some basic scouting. Scouting is the ability to track human scent through the air. Dual-purpose dogs are the most common type of dog Hilliard's team procures for the DOD.

Most dual-purpose dogs are German shepherds, Belgian Malinois, or Dutch shepherds. The shepherds usually hail from Eastern Europe, and the Malinois from the Netherlands and other Western European countries.

The dogs the DOD uses are not usually pedigreed or registered. What the DOD wants is functionality, not pure-breed lines. This can make dogs heartier and less prone to problems. The mixing of breeds is particularly prevalent in the Belgian Malinois.

Want a bigger Malinois? (Malinois have gotten notably larger in recent years.) The breeder won't hesitate to mingle the Malinois with a Great Dane. Want a stronger dog with more reliable nerves than the more reactive and thin-nerved Malinois? Breed the Malinois to a German shepherd. Doc Hilliard says he's also seen very distinctive mixes of Malinois with boxer, boxer–pit bull, and boxer–Bouvier, as well.

At times this intermingling can make for dogs who are exactly on the cusp of one dog breed or the other, and it can be hard to tease apart the dog's background. The difference between calling a dog a Malinois or a German shepherd, for instance, can come down to the type of head the dog has, or the dog's body angles. A more sloped hind end might be the final arbiter in calling the dog a shepherd.

The list of jobs for these dual-purpose dogs is blissfully short compared with the alphabet soup that makes up their single-purpose counterparts' job list. Some say it's best for a dog to have just one job and specialize in it, but most handlers think dual-purpose dogs work just fine.

PEDD (patrol explosive detector dog)—PEDDs are the backbone of the Department of Defense's war-dog program. The dogs are used by MPs and other law enforcement across all services. In addition to sniffing out bombs and doing patrol work, these dogs have some basic scouting abilities.

PNDD (patrol narcotics detector dog)—These dogs are the drug-sniffing counterparts of PEDDs and are also used in the army, the navy, the air force, and the marines.

Multi-purpose canines are the Cairos of the military. They're used by Special Operations personnel. MPC is both a category and a job description. In addition to doing everything PEDDs can do, these super-high-drive dogs can be used in parachute or rappel operations. They sometimes wear waterproof tactical vests, night-vision or infra-red cameras, and other highly specialized canine equipment. They're extremely resilient, environmentally sound, and almost unflappable. As Arod says, "They can do all this and pursue a bad guy through a wall of fire and tear you to pieces if they need to."

11

AND THEN THERE'S LARS . . .

The USS *Norfolk* is a Los Angeles-class fast-attack submarine reeking of the paint being smoothed onto its surface to keep it black and in stealth mode when deployed. This submarine does serious business.

So why on this hot, sunny July afternoon are people on the dock and on the deck of the sub laughing? "That is hilarious!" chuckles the burly chief of the boat (COB), Senior Chief Machinist Mate Sean Craycraft. Others are smiling and pointing and taking pictures. The source of their mirth? Lars J274, a fifteen-pound Jack Russell terrier, a wiry seaman, and a master of tight spaces.

"Fear the terriers!" cries a sailor, and everyone laughs some more. Dog handler Navy Master-at-Arms Third Class Cameron Frost hasn't even had Lars for two weeks, but he's used to his canine partner drawing this kind of jibe, and he has a ready answer. "I've already ordered my Coach bag to carry him in."

Lars was supposed to be a drug dog, but there was a mix-up at dog school, and he got trained as an explosive detector dog (EDD) instead. That suits him fine. He's a self-confident, assertive dog with a detectable swagger.

Frost joined the navy because more than anything else in the world he wanted to be a dog handler. From early on in his enlistment he cleaned kennels, fed dogs, did whatever work kennel masters needed done, in order to show how badly he wanted to work with dogs.

Three years later his hard work paid off, and he got to attend the handler course at Lackland Air Force Base. He thrived on the rigors of combat training with German shepherds and Belgian Malinois. When he returned to his home base at the naval weapons station in Yorktown, he was assigned to Rokio L241, a patrol-narcotics German shepherd. They soon deployed to Afghanistan and stayed mostly inside the wire at Bagram Airfield during their deployment. Rokio's accomplishments consisted mainly of finding drugs coming in with the Afghans working on the base. At the end of the tour, Frost and Rokio returned to the United States and Rokio was assigned to another handler.

Frost was not left without a dog, however. About ten days before I met him at Naval Station Norfolk, he had been assigned Lars, who at age seven is something of a veteran in the world of explosives detection. He has a reputation for an excellent nose and a strong drive to do his job.

But Lars will never deploy. He's just too small. A wrong step with a boot could prove disastrous for him.

The navy uses Jack Russells to sniff out drugs and explosives in ships and submarines. Originally bred to be ratters, these terriers thrive on squeezing into small places. A number of these energetic little dogs are sprinkled at naval bases throughout the U.S., including Pearl Harbor.

Lars and his small comrades are never trained as patrol dogs. When your shoulders are about one foot off the ground, there's a limit to how much protection you can offer. But don't tell this to Lars. He may be small in stature, but he's big in attitude.

"Lars has 'little-man syndrome.' Sometimes he can be a real jerk," Frost says as he hoists him out of his kennel in a navy police SUV and holds him in the crook of his arm. "Don't try to take his food bowl unless you have a hose, because he will attack you. Even if you stick your boot toward the kennel, if the bowl is in there he will attack the boot. See all these bite marks on my boot? These are all from Lars."

Getting Lars's food bowl out of his kennel requires having a hose handy. Like many of his fellow terriers, Lars does not care for getting wet. Just the sight of the hose is enough to make Lars run to the other side of the kennel while someone grabs the food bowl and closes the kennel door.

But his distaste for water does not extend to water bottles. He is a dog obsessed. Empty bottles, full bottles, crushed-beyond-recognition bottles. If he finds one while searching for explosives, "he's done until you take it away and he calms down," explains Frost. He'll chew it, throw it, drag it, make it make as much noise as possible. Clearly, this is not a good trait in a combat situation, where silence can mean the difference between life and death.

Lars stands out wherever he goes when he's on duty. He has been on several presidential missions, helping to ensure that no one planted explosives before the commander in chief arrives. He recently spent a week in New York City on duty for the UN

General Assembly. He's the short guy on these missions, Frost says. "There's German shepherds. There's Labs. There's Belgian Malinois. And then there's Lars."

It's clear from the reaction dockside at the USS *Norfolk* that Jack Russells are not common vessel inspectors. In fact, Craycraft says that in his twenty-one years on subs this is the first time he's come across a little terrier as a military working dog. The dogs who check for drugs or explosives are usually German shepherds. But shepherds weigh about eighty pounds; you can't just pass one down the ladder, as you can with Lars. Bigger dogs must be securely harnessed (at Norfolk they use hardy harnesses from K9 Storm, a Canadian company that supplies highly specialized equipment to military and police dogs) and lowered down the twenty to thirty feet by rope. Sometimes, a makeshift pulley system is used. The dogs' legs are nestled in a sack of sorts so they don't flail around and hurt themselves.

Perhaps Lars's greatest achievement to date—he has yet to find a bomb—is that he is saving the backs of countless handlers and sub crews. He does wear a harness, but it's just his standard-issue gear. During his twenty-foot descent, he appears more like a stuffed toy than a military working dog. Frost stands on top of the submarine and passes him down to a crew member, who is waiting for the dog with outstretched arms, balancing on a narrow rim several feet down. This sort of handoff goes on until Lars reaches the bottom.

I wonder why someone didn't just take Lars under his arm for the descent, but it quickly becomes evident when I try to go down the ladder.

It is not your standard steep marine ladder. The main ladder of the USS *Norfolk* is straight up-and-down, shiny steel without even the slightest angle to it. This is my first descent into the belly of a nuclear sub, and I can't help remembering a cross-country plane trip a few weeks earlier. I sat next to a retired navy submarine engineer who still does contract work for the navy. He told me that back in the day, a bunch of crew members had gone out and gotten snockered. As his pal started down the ladder afterward, he missed a step, or didn't hang on tight enough, and plummeted thirty feet down to the bottom. His back never recovered.

By the time I get to the bottom, Lars is trotting past officers in quiet meetings and crew members who point and laugh and follow. He is a scruffy pied piper, gathering submariners as he moves jauntily through the sub. Once in the berthing area, Frost and Lars get to work.

Frost, seemingly unfazed by the amusement of his audience, lifts his partner from one stripped bunk to the next. Lars's nose checks three levels of bunks, plus floor and ceiling. Sometimes Lars shows interest, and Frost releases him and lets him sniff around a bunk on a long leather leash. A few minutes into the exercise, Lars scrambles from Frost's hands and onto a top bunk. He makes a beeline up the gray-and-white striped mattress to the pillow. After a quick sniff of the pillow, he sits and looks expectantly at Frost. He has found his quarry, an explosive (sans detonator) under a pillow. The onlookers cheer and applaud.

Frost hurls out an enthusiastic and high-pitched, "Good boy, Lars!" and throws a yellow squeaky ball to the top berth. Lars catches it and the tiny quarters fill with *squeak squeak* as he wags and bites his prize. Down the passageway at their meeting, the officers have to wonder what is going on.

We make our way back to the ladder, and when I next see Lars, he is on the dock, being laughed at by a whole new group of sailors. Frost takes it in stride. "Goes with the territory," he says and shrugs. Lars jumps his front paws up on Frost's leg, wags, and stares at him. Frost leans down and scratches Lars behind the ears. "You're a good boyyyy," he says in a hushed tone. Frost may not admit it in public, but it's clear that Lars, small as he is, is growing on him.

12

ONLY THE BOLD WITH
AN *UNNATURAL* DESIRE

Even Lars had to pass a buy team's muster once upon a time. In order to be considered for any MWD job, dogs undergo careful scrutiny.

The dogs being screened must be between twelve and thirty-six months old (the older ones generally have more training) and need to be in excellent health, with no acute or chronic conditions that would be costly to treat. In addition, buyers evaluate behavior, temperament, and trainability. If anything's amiss, it's the equivalent of a human draftee's flat feet or color blindness.

The testing takes place outdoors and indoors. Indoors is not posh: Depending on the location, it can be a barn, garage, or even a large tent. There needs to be some furniture, like drawers and old couches, but otherwise it's pretty bare bones.

Since no matter how healthy a dog is or how good he is at basics like being interested in a ball or performing a good bite, if a military working dog is skittish and balky from the get-go, he won't fare well in the dog program. Bombs and ammo and thin nerves don't mix, so the first tests given are preliminary environmental stability tests.

Here's the official Department of Defense standard, from the *Statement of Work: Potential Military Working Dogs, 341st Training Squadron*:

> *Testing of the potential detector dog begins with introducing the dog to a complex environment while walked on leash by a DOD handler. Ideally, this environment is unfamiliar to the dog and features a number of intense stimuli that can be used to test the animal's environmental stability, or "boldness." Stimuli of interest include tight spaces such as closets and cabinets, slick floors, elevated footing, obstacles, stairs, noisy and startling objects, and groups of people. Any and all such stimuli may be used at the Evaluators' discretion to assess the stability and "boldness" of dogs presented to DOD for possible purchase. The dog will not be played with or stimulated with a reward object (e.g., Kong or ball) during this testing. To be eligible for DOD purchase, the dog shall behave boldly and fearlessly. If the animal is momentarily fearful, it may still be considered for purchase if it recovers quickly and if it displays sufficient willingness to confront stressful stimuli when coaxed. DOD will not accept dogs that are consistently or severely fearful or shy or retiring; that are noise-sensitive; that are strongly aggressive to handlers or bystanders and other neutral parties; or that refuse to negotiate obstacles such as stairs or slick floors.*

It doesn't sound like it would be too hard to find dogs who fit the bill. Jake would pass this part of the test without a problem. This ninety-pound mellow yellow Lab has nerves of steel. He sleeps through earthquakes, will walk or run on any surface (especially if there's something delectable to eat or to roll on as a goal), and has never flinched during the very loud fireworks people set off on our nearby beach for the Fourth of July and the Lunar New Year.

The only thing he's ever been scared of is the Golden Gate Bridge. The vibrations made him pull away once when we were in full tourist mode with some visiting friends. But as soon as I brought out some dog treats, he forgot all about the fact that he was vibrating more than two hundred feet above the cold, unforgiving ocean waters and marched on like the brave and always-hungry soldier he is.

 Jake—Passes the environmental stability test with ease.

★

Medical evaluations come later on the test day, with vet techs drawing blood from candidates who are temperamentally suited to the job, and vets examining the dogs, and sometimes even anesthetizing an occasional dog in order to take X-rays of the hips, elbows, and lumbar spine. (X-rays happen only after a dog has passed all behavioral testing.) Dysplasia and other structural abnormalities have done in many a military working dog, so even though vendors have often already submitted radiographs, vets may want to do their own. Besides a thorough medical check, dogs who will be doing patrol work need to have good teeth and jaws, with all four canine teeth present and in excellent condition. The better to bite bad guys with . . .

Jake may or may not have passed the physical evaluation. He has no major health issues at all, but he has always been the owner of a set of funky hips. Shortly after we adopted him at six months old, we noticed that he ran like a sack of potatoes whenever at the beach or Golden Gate Park. We eventually had him X-rayed and were told he might have hip issues down the road. We're nine years down that road, and it's been an adventure filled with running and jumping and living life to the fullest. So far, he's OK. So for argument's sake, we'll say Jake would pass the medical portion of the test.

 Jake—Passes the physical, but will need his hips reexamined quickly if anything becomes a problem.

★

Next up on test day, all dogs get evaluated for drive in retrieving and detection. For dual-purpose dogs, the team will also look for drive and competence and confidence in biting. It's now time for dogs to have a ball—and an arm or leg, for dogs who will be patrolling. We'll move inside the big, drafty barn for this portion.

Most dogs have been taught by breeders to covet a ball or a Kong toy. The majority of dogs have come to love their Kong, even if they weren't born with a natural drive to obsess over it. Breeders work to boost interest in dogs who would rather just sit outside and stare at butterflies. The reason this is important is because it's the rubber Kong toy that most trainers and handlers will use as a reward, and in order for a dog to want to do various tasks, he's going to want to know there's pay at the end. Pay for a military working dog is a Kong or a ball, or anything the handler lets him bite. And of course, great praise from the handler.

The dogs being tested generally have little to no training in detection work. Detection at this evaluation stage is much simpler than actually seeking out explosives or drugs. It really comes to a dog's desire to play with a ball and to search for a ball he can't see. Testers show the dog the ball and then hide it (usually in one of those drawers mentioned earlier) and watch to see how much the dog wants to find it. The evaluators are looking for a dog who wants the ball so much that he's clearly thinking about it even if he can't see it, and he's excited and will search tirelessly and intensively until he locates the ball. You can imagine the energy a dog like this has.

Once the dog has the ball, Doc and the team look at how jealously he guards the ball in order to keep it, and how enduring and vigorous his interest is in playing with the ball. In essence, the dog has to have a passionate desire to have a toy in his mouth and a very strong olfactory search drive in order to pass this part of the test.

"It's actually an unnatural desire to play with an object. It's a specially bred mutated form of hunting behavior, selected for by dog breeders over hundreds of years," according to Doc Hilliard. "Every dog we're looking for needs to have it."

✓ *Jake—Barely passes the ball test. He loves the ball and will search for it tirelessly, but once he has the ball, he is happy to share it with whoever wants it. Doc says it's not ideal, but that the possessiveness can be trained into him, at least to an extent. Our now-deceased springer spaniel, Nisha, was completely ball obsessed, and if you tried to take a ball from her, you had to be prepared to do battle.*

★ ★ ★ 13 ★ ★ ★

THE WRONG STUFF

B ut it's hard to judge every dog's passion for the ball. Sometimes a dog goes to the United States and passes through
training, only to fail in advanced training school.

I watched an army dog and his handler, who would be deploying to Afghanistan in a matter of weeks, as they tried to work on
exercises at the Inter-Service Advanced Skills K-9 (IASK) Course,
at the Yuma Proving Ground in Arizona. The dog was listless and
didn't seem to want to do the exercises. The ball didn't mean much
to him when he got it. He'd take it for a few seconds and drop it.
Part of it may have been the heat (114 degrees Fahrenheit), but some
of the problem was simply that he didn't care enough about the ball
to go through the rigors of this level of training. The man in charge
of the course, Gunnery Sergeant Kristopher Knight, said he could
tell when he first saw the dog that the dog didn't care enough about
the reward.

"If I made you run three klicks in this heat and told you 'OK,
now do what I tell you and I'll give you this nice cold water,' you'd

do just about anything for that water at that point. *That's* how a strong dog feels about his toy. *That's* the passion this dog lacks." The dog did not end up deploying and is working with his handler on trying to improve his love for his "paycheck." If that doesn't work, he will no longer be a soldier dog.

The buy team also makes time to test an innate skill that's vital to a good sniffer dog: how quickly a dog can learn to associate a ball with a weird odor. It's the cornerstone of detection training, and once at dog school in the United States, dogs have only sixty days to master detect eight explosives scents, so the team does not want slow learners. How does a dog come to associate a ball with an odor?

Doc or someone on the team gets a dog searching for her ball inside the barn. Suddenly the dog hits this weird-smelling scent she's probably never encountered before. Testers used to use substances like marijuana or potassium chlorate, but these days they don't want to expose a dog to narcotics or drugs so early in the game. There's a chance it could confuse a dog if, for example, she was exposed to marijuana during testing and went on to become an explosives detector. There's a lot of weed in Afghanistan, and you don't want an explosives dog alerting to it. This olfactory separation is even more important for narcotics dogs. If a drug dog alerts to that early memory of potassium chlorate, but handlers think she's found a stash of drugs, it could be a very big problem.

The scent that the team uses for testing could be something as simple as vanilla or licorice, which Doc refers to as "arbitrary odors." When the dog, who is looking for her ball, hits this new odor, all sorts of things happen. The dog thinks, "I've never smelled this before!" and shows a tiny change of behavior, perhaps stopping or wagging or tilting her head. At that moment, someone throws the ball so it lands right on the source of the odor, and the dog is cheered on for her "feat."

This happens a few more times, placing the odor in various places in the room and having a ball "magically" land on it when the dog successfully sniffs the odor. Many dogs learn extremely rapidly to associate an odor and a ball. The odor becomes a totem for the ball. It's a Pavlovian process that works wonders. Once they are at dog school, it becomes the way dogs once again begin associating scents with a reward—only the scents at school will be the real deal and not something you'd find in Granny's pantry.

Dogs who will do patrol work have more testing ahead of them. This is something the breeders and their trainers have worked on extensively. The dogs need to show aggression in response to a decoy (a human posing as a "bad guy") dressed without obvious bite equipment, and they must show great interest in biting and holding decoys who are wearing bite sleeves. The bites need to be strong and full, and the dog has to hold steady while biting, even if under threat. The type of bite is important. A shallow, weak, or shifting bite (in which the dog does something known as "typewriting") is not desirable and could be cause for elimination.

The buy team's goal is to buy sixty to one hundred dogs per visit to Europe; some dogs will go to the TSA's detector dog program, the rest to the Department of Defense's dog school at Lackland, for basic training. Once the dogs have been chosen, they tend not to stick around with the vendors for long.

Let's say the team finishes at the barn site, where members

selected several dogs. Often within hours, the dogs are packed up and driven via truck to Frankfurt, where they are taken out of shipping crates, walked, and their crates cleaned. There, they wait for the eleven- or twelve-hour flight to Houston, which they'll make in the cargo hold of a commercial airliner. Once the dogs land, they're put in an air-conditioned truck for a three-hour drive to Lackland. They're met by handlers, veterinarians, and technicians at Lackland's Medina base kennels. The dogs—who have been on the road for between two and six days, depending on transportation availability—are unloaded and given a cursory exam.

Veterinarians at Lackland occasionally find dogs arriving from overseas to be underweight and to harbor skin, ear, or other infections. It's surprising, because the buy teams would have seen the dogs from two to six days earlier. The teams tend not to take dogs with these problems, because, as Doc Hilliard says, "we don't subsidize neglect of dogs." The problems are treatable, but if you're going to spend thousands of dollars on a dog, you would hope that the dog would have been given adequate kibble and care before arriving.

On a visit to the Medina clinic, one of the many dogs I saw being checked out was Lobo R705. He was a long-haired black shepherd, but you could hardly tell. He had received a buzz cut the previous week in order to get rid of the badly matted fur he arrived with from the vendor in Europe. Under the mats his entire chest had been bright red and inflamed from urine burns. He also had a raging ear infection. A veterinarian prescribed a regimen of antibiotic salves and ear meds. Upon recheck, Lobo's skin had healed, as had his ears. A staffer congratulated him. "Good job, boy!"

Of course, many of these freshly arrived dogs don't speak English; that is, they don't know English commands, so trainers may start saying things like *"Bravver hund!"* (Good dog!) or *"Aus!"* (Let go!). Eventually the dogs learn English. The only vestige of their foreign tongue may soon be their name.

★ ★ ★ 14 ★ ★ ★

WHAT'S IN A NAME?

Dogs are named by their breeders, so when you're among military working dogs who hail from the kinds of places these dogs do, it is not surprising to hear names like Patja, Fritz, Pasha, Frenke, Caffu, Biko, Banzi, or Wolka. Or Fenji.

But the most common four dog names across the services, I found out after the Defense Department did a little digging for me, are Rex, Max, Nero, and Rocky. I know of no dogs in civilian life named Rex (or Fido, for that matter), so it's nice to know that this old-fashioned name, which means "King," is still being used for these noble dogs.

Not all names are so magisterial, though. In fact, dog program administrators and some handlers who are in the loop seem to think that breeders may sit back and chuckle when they name some of their dogs—dogs who will be at the forefront of the war on terror, being called time and time again by whatever name the breeder assigned them. "I'm pretty sure they're messing with us sometimes," says one insider. And a military veterinarian chuckled and shook his head when he told me, "I think they do it on purpose."

This would account for a brave war dog, Davy, whom we've already met. The name wouldn't be a problem, except, as you may recall, Davy is a girl. So is Bob. The gender switching seems to go the other way around most of the time, though, with big, tough boy dogs getting girly names. To wit: Freida, Kitty, and Judy. "Calling him Freida bothered me," former handler John Engstrom said. "It was just wrong."

I've heard stories about two male dogs named Kitty in the military. Both had reputations as very aggressive dogs. Remember Johnny Cash's song "A Boy Named Sue"? Same syndrome, perhaps.

Then there are the awkward names, including a dog named Bad. Talk about sending mixed messages when calling your dog. And let's not forget Sid. "Anytime you said Sid, it sat," Engstrom told me.

It seems that breeders in foreign countries are greatly influenced by American pop culture for kids. Perhaps they even let their children name the dogs. On a list of thousands of military working dog names from the last several years, there are the requisite *Sesame Street* characters, including Ernie, Bert, Elmo, and Oscar. Disney classic animation characters score big, with Mickey, Minnie, Donald, Daisy, Huey, Duey, Louie, Pluto, Goofy, Winnie, Tigger, Baloo, King Louie, Mowgli, Bambi, Beauty, Beast, Belle, Ariel, and Simba. Breeders also borrow from any famous dogs out there, including Snoopy, Benji, Scooby Doo, Toto, and Rin Tin Tin.

Let's not forget the oddball names. Some are embarrassing,

others are just weird. Imagine being downrange in a life-or-death situation and shouting for "Baby Cakes!" "Baby Bear!" "Busty!" or "Moo!" Breeders may have been hungry or thirsty when they named Cheddar, Cherry, Chips, Cider, Coffee, Cookie, Ihop, and Kimchee.

Some names seem to be commentaries on a dog's personality: Bleak, Calamity, Funny, Grief (RIP: he died in Afghanistan not long ago), Grim, and Icky. Wait a minute. Icky?! Time for a serious, calm chat with one's commanding officer about just changing this poor dog's name.

★ ★ ★ 15 ★ ★ ★

BORN IN THE USA

Going to Europe to buy dogs is a necessity, says Doc Hilliard, because there just aren't enough strong military dog candidates in the United States. Thanks to the long tradition of dog sports like Schutzhund and institutions like the Royal Dutch Police Dog Association, Europeans have a deeply entrenched source of dogs cut out for the types of duties military working dogs perform. "I'd love nothing better than to be able to buy American, but the dogs just aren't here," Doc says.

American vendors sell dogs to Lackland in much the same fashion as European vendors do, but because they sell in rather small numbers, the vendors usually go to Lackland with their dogs rather than have a buy team visit. Ironically, most of the dogs the U.S. vendors sell to the Defense Department were purchased in Europe.

The dog program still has a policy of accepting donations from average citizens or breeders. Every now and then, Doc and his people get a phone call from Ma and Pa wanting to donate their German shepherd to protect the U.S. But the odds the dog can pass the tests are astronomically low, he says. The genetics and intensive training just aren't there. The dog program won't take a dog in if it can't use him, so Ma and Pa—if they've come all the way to Lackland even after all the warnings about the testing—will likely end up driving home with their dog, who couldn't meet program standards.

What about shelters? Aren't they filled with dogs who are available for next to nothing and are highly trainable? The British military has been saving the lives of shelter dogs for years, training them and providing them for its armed forces, according to animal scientist John Bradshaw, who has done extensive work with England's Defence Animal Centre in Melton Mowbray, near Leicester. (It is roughly the equivalent of Lackland Air Force Base as far as dog procurement and training goes.)

The Defence Animal Centre also relies heavily on public donations of dogs. There's even a Web site with FAQs for those who want to donate. The Centre is interested in German shepherds, Belgian shepherds, or "gun dog" breeds between the ages of one and three years of age. The intake procedure is relatively easy, and on the Web site there's even space devoted to reassuring potential donors that their dogs will be in good hands:

> *If you are considering donating or selling your dog to us, rest assured that your dog will be cared for, stimulated and trained through positive reward-based training, i.e., plenty of ball work, play and focused games.*
>
> *When you have made the decision to support your country by donating your dog and the dog has passed all the necessary assessments you can rest assured that they are being well cared for. The Defence Animal Centre pledges to endeavour to meet The Five Freedoms:*

- *Freedom from hunger*
- *Freedom from pain, injury and disease*
- *Freedom from fear and distress*
- *Freedom from physical discomfort*
- *Freedom to perform most normal forms of behaviour*

The U.S. Department of Defense has recently begun making limited experiments obtaining dogs from shelters. But this has not proven successful. In the last year, consignment evaluators have been going to shelters in the San Antonio area and looking at hundreds of dogs. Only one has passed. His name is Lucky, and he's a Labrador. The program is not encouraged by the high-labor, low-yield results, so don't expect to see dogs flying out of shelters and into the armed forces in the U.S. anytime soon. Our standards, it seems, are different from those in the UK.

So if we have a desire to procure dogs closer to home but just can't, are there any other options? Yes, and as it turns out, it's the reason anyone who enters Hilliard's building has to dip his or her feet in green disinfectant.

The Defense Department is making its very own Belgian Malinois puppies: Seventy-five were whelped here in 2010, 115 in 2009. The goal is to whelp two hundred puppies a year. About half the puppies won't make the cut, so once the goal is reached, there will be one hundred fewer dogs to buy overseas.

Why the Malinois? Mostly because they tend to be more durable than German shepherds, who are known for their hip, elbow, and back problems. Plus, according to some trainers I've spoken with, it's because the Malinois don't let thinking get in their way. They say that a shepherd will often think about what you tell him to do, or about his situation, but a Malinois just acts as he's trained to. Many prefer this. I don't know if Rin Tin Tin would applaud this rationale, but there's no turning back now. The program has been in place since 1998, at first as an experimental one and now as a full-fledged program, run by Doc Hilliard himself.

We head downstairs from our meeting place to go see the puppies. To get access, we have to dip our soles at another disinfectant station. I'm not allowed to stop in at the whelping kennels to see the newest litter, because I spent the morning in the company of other dogs, and I could end up carrying disease to the vulnerable pups. But I do get to visit a batch of seven-week-old puppies from the pairing of a Netherlands stud named Robbie—who has sired some serious champion working dogs—and a bitch named Heska. Hilliard bought Heska overseas and bred her to Robbie while in the Netherlands. She came to Lackland to be monitored through her pregnancy and have her puppies on U.S. soil.

Her pups are fawn-colored, with downy fur and dark brown/black faces that look up from their exercise pen with a plaintive "Pick me up, please!" expression. Some still have a floppy ear or two, but for the most part, their ears have become upright. They're from the A litter, so every pup's name will start with the letter A. To distinguish puppy-program dogs from other MWDs, all dogs from the puppy program are given double letters to start their name. So this litter is made up of dogs with names like Aangus, Aatlas, and Aalice.

Aalice has caught my eye. She is still floppy-eared, and she appears extremely social, making eye contact and standing with paws propped on the enclosure to get my attention. But since I've been with other dogs earlier in the day, I can't hold her. The pups are still not fully immunized, and it wouldn't be safe.

So Doc Hilliard picks her up instead, and she snuggles right into his arms, and then uses his arms as a place to prop her paw, and starts licking his neck and then up to his jaw and cheek. It's hard for him to carry on the conversation while Aalice is slathering him with such adulation, so he passes her to a staffer who's more than happy to take her off his hands.

Puppies in the puppy program leave Lackland pretty early in life. They're with their mom for several weeks, and then they get placed in foster homes until they're seven months old, when they return to Lackland and go through a sort of puppy preschool to see which ones may have what it takes to become a military working dog.

Ask anyone who has fostered a Malinois puppy, and they'll tell you two things:

1. It's a great way to be an intimate part of helping the military working dog world.

2. Hide your shoes, socks, slippers, and furniture.

There's a reason these pups are nicknamed "malligators." They are all mouth and teeth. Arod has fostered three. "They ate our entire home," he says. He and his family ended up adopting the last one, Ttrina, after she didn't make the cut as a military working dog. Despite her propensity to malligator herself around the house, they took her in because they'd grown attached to her—teeth and all.

The puppy program is always looking for foster homes. To

qualify, volunteers have to live within three hours of San Antonio so they can drive back for monthly appointments. A fenced yard is ideal. Fosters have to disclose how many other pets they have and what kind. "If you have five cats, we need to know that," says David Garcia, dog program foster consultant. "We'll find you a low-drive dog that will be a better fit."

Foster homes aren't expected to do formal training. That's what dog school is for. But they do help a puppy become comfortable with various environments and stimuli, such as busy streets, stairs, loud vacuums, and crowds. Fosters can also work on increasing a dog's desire to find a toy or a training treat; this is good for future training, when finding objects is a dog's core mission.

When I met with Garcia, he was in a slight panic. He needed to find twelve homes for the A litter (Aalice and her brothers and sisters) within two weeks. It wasn't looking good. The program had just expanded the distance limits for foster homes in order to include Austin residents, but word hadn't gotten out yet. Garcia was going to be calling some previous repeat fosters and was planning on attending a puppy expo as well.

"Once you see them and know them, they're pretty hard to resist," he says. He adds that it's not *that* hard to puppy-proof a home. And he talks about how gratifying it can be to raise a puppy who will go on to save the lives of servicemen and -women. "It's not every day you get to raise a future hero."

Doc and his staff are investing heavily in making the puppy program a success. They've bought some frozen sperm from sought-after studs and also brought back a male named Arnold, who they hope will father some great pups. When Hilliard and staff go to Europe on future trips, he says they'll be looking for some "interesting" dogs for breeding.

They recently purchased a female Malinois puppy named Boudin, whose dad is Robbie (Aalice's father) and mom is Kyra (pronounced Keera). The pairing of Robbie and Kyra has produced some very successful working dogs in Europe. Doc wants the Military Working Dog Program to have some of this bloodline, some of these champion genetics, so the puppy program bought Boudin and a full brother named Bruno. Both are registered pedigree dogs. (They will not be paired, for obvious reasons.)

As a rule, Doc doesn't like to get registered pedigree Malinois, because he thinks they don't deal with stress as well as non-pedigreed dogs and because they tend to be smaller and less robust, more susceptible to stress. But these dogs are different, he hopes. I spent a few hours one afternoon with eight-week-old Boudin at her brand-new foster home near Lackland, with her foster dad, Air Force Technical Sergeant Joe Null. Despite her crazy puppy energy and frequent and high-pitched barking, she looks like she has the makings of an excellent dog: She's strong, has a committed bite when playing with a tug toy, and doesn't give up when hunting for a Kong.

But there's more to becoming a military working dog than getting bred or drafted. That's the easy part. Making it through the rigors of dog school is another matter altogether. Some dogs might decide to be draft dodgers if they knew what was up next.

A TATTOO, AND
A LITTLE OPERATION

Veterinarian Ronnie Nye, a retired army lieutenant colonel, has an easygoing, friendly manner that would put most human patients at ease if he were an MD. But Fred, a Netherlands-born German shorthaired pointer, looks like he would rather be somewhere else. His stub of a tail stays tucked down even as Nye strokes him and tells him with a confident, knowing smile that it's going to be all right.

After an injection of a cocktail of sedatives, Fred appears a little drunk and within a couple of minutes slumps into the waiting arms of a vet assistant, who helps steady him onto the stainless-steel operating table. When Fred is completely out, assistants turn him onto his back, withdraw some urine from his bladder via a needle and syringe, put an endotracheal tube down his throat for anesthesia, and secure his paws to the table with ties. His floppy ears, splayed out on the steel, make an easy surface for the vet tech, who spends about twenty minutes tattooing his assigned number (R739) on the underside of his left ear. As her tattoo pen buzzes away, Nye shaves the dog's stomach, vacuums the loose fur off the dog, isolates the incision area with blue surgical drapes, and poises a scalpel over Fred's bare belly. . . .

Won't hurt a bit.

★ ★ ★ 17 ★ ★ ★

BOOT CAMP

The world's largest dog school—aka the Department of Defense Military Working Dog School, 341st Training Squadron— lies on a flat, featureless chunk of land on the outskirts of San Antonio, at Lackland Air Force Base. Sprawled out on nearly seven thousand arid acres, Lackland is a place for newcomers. Each year, thirty-five thousand air force recruits come here for basic training.

Also among Lackland's newcomers every year are the 340 relatively young dogs who will be trained as military working dogs and the 460 two-legged students who come through Lackland to learn the basics of dog handling.

The boot camp program where trainers build military working dogs from the ground up is referred to as dog school. The program that teaches handler skills is called the handler course. Pretty much all soldier dogs and handlers across the military are trained here. (The exceptions are Special Operations dogs and dogs for the IDD and TEDD programs, which are dedicated to a faster turnaround time for certain explosives detector dogs. These dogs are trained by contractors.)

Dogs who are selected to go the dual-purpose route—and that's the vast majority of the dogs—will have a total of 120 days to learn all the skills necessary to certify in explosives or narcotics detection as well as patrol work. Single-purpose detection-only dogs do it in about 90. Contrary to what many on the outside think, with the exception of a couple of smaller programs (combat tracking dogs and specialized search dogs), dogs are not matched up with handlers at Lackland; they're assigned to handlers once they're shipped to the bases that request them.

But before the dogs can even start to get the rigorous training they need in order to one day become soldier dogs, they have to go through a rather grueling initial time at Lackland—one that may make boot camp for their two-legged friends look like a walk in the park.

Every soldier, sailor, airman, and marine must go through some form of induction when entering the military. A haircut, health exams, reams of paperwork—all the less glamorous aspects of serving one's country need to be taken care of before getting down to the business of boot camp.

Soldier dogs go through a more rigorous induction process, including time on the operating table. The road to becoming a military working dog entails being poked, prodded, cut open, sealed shut, and wearing a bucket around your head for a few days.

After a ten-day quarantine, during which they're visually evaluated every two hours, the dogs get physicals, blood work, vaccinations, and flea and heartworm treatments. The rest of a dog's induction is done under full anesthesia. Female dogs get spayed, males with undescended testicles get neutered. (The U.S. has one of the few militaries that will purchase these "cryptorchid" dogs.) But otherwise males generally remain intact. The thinking is that these dogs are more aggressive and primed for action with those hormones coursing through their bodies. Also on the list of induction events: Both sexes get their tattoo number inked into the inside of their left ear while anesthetized.

And these days, every dog over thirty-five pounds also undergoes a potentially lifesaving surgery called a gastropexy. The surgery will prevent a syndrome known as bloat from becoming fatal. Not long ago, 9 percent of U.S. military working dog losses resulted from complications of bloat. That number has dropped to zero since all large dogs started getting "pexied," as it's called in soldier dog circles.

Bloat, aka gastric dilation-volvulus, is a dangerous condition that mainly affects large, deep-chested dogs—precisely the kind the military favors. Bloat occurs when the stomach becomes overdistended with gas for any of a variety of reasons—not all known. This alone can be deadly, since it can cut off normal circulation when the enlarged stomach presses against major veins. Respiration can also be affected, since the stomach is pressing against the lungs. If you ever ate way too much in one sitting and found it hard to take a good breath, you'll have a feel for what the beginning of that phase of bloat can feel like.

But it's when the stomach twists at both ends (at the top the esophagus and at the bottom the pyloric valve) that bloat becomes especially lethal. Gas in the stomach can no longer escape either way, and circulation is severely impaired, leaving irreversible cell damage. Shock and cardiac arrest can occur within hours without emergency treatment.

On a visit to Lackland's brand-new Medina Military Working

Dog Clinic—so new you can still smell the happy scent of paint over the scent of dog—I watch Nye operate on his reluctant patient. He has done at least four hundred of these surgeries in the last few years. Fred may not realize it, but he is in good hands.

As Michael Jackson's "Ben" cuts through the static of the radio that's propped up on a shelf, Nye makes the incision. It's only about three inches long. The surgery will take no more than an hour, and in the end, Fred's stomach will be sutured to his ventral abdominal wall. His chances of dying of bloat will have been virtually eliminated.

Nye stitches Fred's abdomen, the dog's paws are unstrapped, tubes are withdrawn, and Fred is taken back to a recovery kennel. He will be checked frequently to make sure the Rimadyl and opiates he's getting are keeping the pain at bay and that the incision is healing well.

To keep Fred's mouth and teeth from exploring the surgery site, and to prevent his back paws from scratching at his fresh tattoo, Fred will wear a bucket over his head for the next several days. It's an old, scratched-up, dark blue plastic bucket with the bottom cut out, and it's fitted with ties that secure it to his collar so he won't be able to get it off. Not exactly the traditional "Elizabethan" collar civilian dogs wear after surgical procedures, but Fred doesn't mind.

Air Force Staff Sergeant Richard Crotty was stationed in Iraq when he got in touch with me. He wanted to relate this story of his first working dog, Ben B190, a German shepherd.

For seven months in 2006 Crotty and Ben served at the Eskan

Village Air Base in Saudi Arabia, with the Sixty-fourth Expeditionary Security Forces Squadron. Their main duties were to search vehicles, conduct foot patrols, and participate in random antiterrorism exercises in support of Operation Iraqi Freedom. They lived the life of expats, in a villa on base where they could have Chinese food or pizza delivered. Ben spent most nights on Crotty's bed. It was the good life for the pair, who preferred being together nearly 24/7 to life in the States, where dogs have to spend most of their days and nights in kennels.

They returned to Cannon Air Force Base in New Mexico in August 2006, and Ben's nights were once again spent in kennels. Crotty missed the camaraderie of those days and nights in Saudi Arabia, but he knew there was nothing he could do to keep his dog with him Stateside. On the night of January 7, 2007, Crotty went to say good night to Ben in his kennel and found Ben lying on his side—something the dog never did. When Crotty went to pet him, Ben urinated. Crotty noticed that the dog's stomach was rock hard—a sign he could have bloat. Ben had not had prophylactic gastropexy. Most male dogs back then hadn't.

With no time to lose, Crotty picked Ben up, put him in a patrol truck, and raced to the vet, sirens blaring. The immediate diagnosis called for emergency surgery. As he looked down at his dog on the operating table, Crotty's eyes were so filled with tears that "I could not see him as I was looking down. It was like it was my child. When the vet finally cut him open, the floor turned completely red."

It was too much. Crotty left the operating room. "When my kennel master came out of the operating room, he just shook his

Sergeant Stubby, World War I hero, lives on at the Smithsonian's National Museum of American History. MARIA GOODAVAGE

This photo from World War II's Battle of Peleliu is a favorite of former Vietnam dog handler Robert Kollar. To him there's something about the handler, Marine Corporal William Scott, and his Doberman pinscher, Prince, that captures everything about the bond between wartime handler and dog. NATIONAL ARCHIVES

Dog alerts to the scent of a homemade explosive (HME) at the Inter-Service Advanced Skills K-9 (IASK) Course in Yuma, Arizona. JARED DORT

The author "catching" a dog at Lackland Air Force Base—Ground Zero for dog and handler training. ROBIN JERSTAD

A new dog draftee at Lackland wears a bucket around his head after undergoing surgery that will prevent the fatal effects of a syndrome called bloat. The bucket keeps him from interfering with the surgical site. ROBIN JERSTAD

Navy Master-at-Arms Second Class Joshua Raymond and Rex P233 learn to work off leash together for the first time at the IASK course. It's a potentially life-saving capability that enables dogs to follow their noses better, and it keeps handlers and others farther from explosives. MARIA GOODAVAGE

Marine Gunnery Sergeant Kristopher Knight, who runs the IASK course, gives Raymond some tips on searching for IEDs. MARIA GOODAVAGE

Raid exercises at the IASK course take place in very realistic settings and come with loud sounds of ammo, IED, and mortar blasts. JARED DORT

"If this doesn't prepare you for Afghanistan, nothing will," Air Force Technical Sergeant Adam Miller says of the IASK course. On this day, in 114-degree heat, Miller has to carry his dog, Tina M111, to safety after she was "shot" during an exercise. JARED DORT

What's in a name? Ask Davy N532, a female dog whose name does not match her gender. Oddball names are not uncommon among military working dogs, whose breeders, usually from Europe, name them. "I trust her with my life. If I didn't trust her, I wouldn't be here," Army Staff Sergeant Marcus Bates says of his Belgian Malinois, Davy N532, during their deployment in Afghanistan. MARCUS BATES

You don't have to be a big dog to be a soldier dog. Lars J274, a Jack Russell terrier with a Napoleon complex, is the perfect size for sniffing out bombs in submarines. U.S. NAVY PHOTO BY PETTY OFFICER SECOND CLASS PAUL D. WILLIAMS

Lars's handler lifts him from bunk to bunk on the USS *Norfolk* so his nose can get close enough to detect explosives on any level. U.S. NAVY PHOTO BY PETTY OFFICER SECOND CLASS PAUL D. WILLIAMS

A "training aid" dog and his handler-in-training start the day enjoying the shade at the Department of Defense Military Working Dog School, at Lackland Air Force Base. ROBIN JERSTAD

head. I lost it right there. My best friend for the last two years was gone."

In the end, the cause of Ben's fatal condition was not bloat. The vet had found inflammation of many organs, which had caused internal bleeding. Crotty was never told the reason for Ben's death, and he's not sure the veterinarian ever figured it out.

★ ★ ★ **18** ★ ★ ★

HANDLERS WITH BUCKETS

S tudents enrolled in the handler course at Lackland have paid their dues typically for months, but sometimes years, helping around kennels at their bases, cleaning poop, working the dogs, assisting handlers with their duties, and generally proving to their field commanders and kennel masters that they are devoted.

Nearly all students in the handler course are military police. They've had to go through some intensive training in order to get to become MPs (or MAs—masters-at-arms—in the navy, or security forces in the air force). But little can prepare them for one of their first exercises:

Pretending that an old .40-caliber metal ammo can is actually a dog.

For three days or so.

In front of all their classmates and anyone else who walks by.

These cans are referred to as buckets—not to be confused with the bucket that Fred had to wear over his head. The buckets were once used to safely transport ammunition, but now, through the magic of the imagination, and the embarrassment of the majority of the students in the class, they have been transformed into dogs.

The buckets are shaped sort of like extra tall shoe boxes and are usually olive or khaki colored. They have two handles at the top and sometimes writing or lettering on the side. They look nothing whatsoever like dogs.

But that's the whole point. Just as medical students don't start out operating on living humans, handler students don't begin their training with a real live dog. It's too risky for the dogs and the students.

The real dogs the handlers train with aren't actually military working dogs, either. These dogs are "training aids." They live at Lackland and are assigned to handler classes throughout the year. Most training-aid dogs are here because they didn't quite cut it as working military dogs. Some washed out of dog school but are perfectly good as canine partners at the school. Others may have already served overseas or at their home bases but, for health or behavioral reasons, cannot work as fully functioning working dogs in the field. Even though they're not deployable, they're valuable assets to the military, and the dog program doesn't want any green handlers messing them up.

By the time they meet their buckets, the students have already gone through a few days of classroom work. These are small, intimate groupings, with twelve students maximum per class. They get plenty of hands-on time with three stuffed German shepherd toy dogs, learning the very basics, like how to put choke collars on them the right way, how to talk to them, and some basic commands. The dogs, though, are stuck in the sitting position, get knocked down easily, and get dirty far too quickly for anything more than classroom training. Since function is far more important than form around here, the buckets are dragged out for the next step in training handlers.

Handlers name their buckets to make these exercises more realistic. Brandon Liebert, the former marine dog handler we met earlier in the book, called his bucket Cananine (pronounced Can-a-nine) because it was a can and it had a 9 spray-painted on the side. "It helped make it a little more believable that this was a dog," he says.

The idea is to do with the buckets just about everything handlers would normally do in the beginning stages of working with a canine training aid. Students have to tell the buckets to sit and lie down; they put two collars on their bucket's handles, making sure they have the choke chain going in the right direction and learning how to change from a dual collar to just a choke. They learn to keep proper safety distance from other students' buckets. They even do drill movements (for those not in the military, that's the "left *face*" business)—no easy feat with a bucket, or a dog.

One of the first things students are taught when working with these military working buckets is how to offer praise. Genuine, heartfelt praise is essential to building a bond between dog and handler. In the working world of these dogs, you don't just say "Good boy!" in a slightly enthusiastic tone. You go crazy for the great deed the dog has done. Your voice goes up at least an octave, often more, just about as high as you can get it and not sound squeaky. You talk fast, and the vowels of your words are pulled longer, and sometimes you're not even understandable, and you're so enthusiastic that if you had a tail it would be wagging like mad. Many experienced handlers even throw in a "Woooo!" At Lackland, the trainers of new

MWDs often add an exuberant "Yeeeehawwwww, hoooo dogggyyyyyyy!" in cowboy fashion. And for extra emphasis, on occasion, "Touch*down* Texas!"

When in the presence of handlers and trainers working their dogs—as opposed to buckets—you'll sometimes hear what sounds like the most enthusiastic praise, but then you realize that the words are all wrong. The tone is thrilled, but instead of words like "What a good boyyyy! Great fiiiiiiiiiiind!" they go something to the effect of "Oh my goddddd! How come you took so long to find that, you little dummy?!" It's a handler's way of expressing a little frustration while the dog remains encouraged about his efforts.

Talking to a real dog with such gusto can take some getting used to. Praising a bucket in such a fashion makes for a real challenge.

"A lot of students get embarrassed. They get red-faced. Some get real quiet, even if they didn't start out that way," says Air Force Technical Sergeant Justin Marshall, instructor supervisor at Lackland. "We let them know that every single canine handler out there right now has gone through this. That seems to help a little."

And heaven forbid a bucket gets loose. Someone yells out "loose dog," and everyone who hears it has to repeat it so everyone else can know what exactly is going on. Handlers who have a bucket on leash have to choke up (grab as close to the leash clasp as possible) on the leash. If the leashed bucket were a real dog, the handlers would then have to put their dog's face in their crotch area so the dog wouldn't see the loose dog coming, and therefore would likely not react aggressively. (Military working dogs are often aggressive with each other, and fights can break out in an instant. Practicing these maneuvers with buckets is best for everyone's sake.)

Bucket training goes on until the students all seem to have a firm grasp of techniques. It usually takes two or three days. At the end, there's a friendly competition in which students try to make the fewest mistakes in handling their buckets. The prize is a good one: The winner gets to choose which real dog he will be working with for the detection portion of the handler course. Other students can decide on their dogs based on how they ranked in the game, but sometimes instructors match students with dogs themselves, especially if they feel a student will do better with a certain type of dog personality. (A timid handler and an extra-bold, assertive dog may not make the best pairing, for instance.)

The buckets are stored away for the next class, and the bucket graduates head to the kennels to get their dogs. Most students are thrilled to finally be working with a flesh-and-blood dog. But for a few—usually those who had little experience with dogs before—it can be daunting. "Some just get scared when they get to the kennel and have to get the dog out. They feel overwhelmed, especially if the dog is really excited," says Marshall. Buckets don't spin in mad circles, and they don't accidentally bite you or bark until your eardrums throb. The energy of these dogs can prove too much for these students, and they turn in their leash shortly after being introduced to their dog.

For the most part, the dogs who work as training aids are old hands at this. They've done this before, sometimes many times before, and some almost seem to try to help students get through the training: "C'mon, just follow me, and I'll find the explosive and I'll make you look good, pal. Then you praise me up and give me my Kong and we'll be square."

For the remainder of the handler course, the dogs will help

their students learn the basics of dog handling. Collars will inevitably be pulled too tight, commands won't be clear, students will balk or move the wrong way when doing bite training, but the dogs persevere. They're happy to be out of their kennels and working. They relish a handler's enthusiasm and praise, and the Kong or ball they get whenever there's a job well done, and the daily, long grooming/bonding sessions from their temporary assignment.

Most students make it through the eleven-week program. By graduation, a couple of students may already have the makings of scars from when a body part was in the wrong place at the wrong time. Seasoned handlers usually have several, all with good stories attached.

Graduation is held in a large fluorescently lit auditorium with mustard-colored walls. On the walls are photographs of handlers who died in the line of duty—a somber reminder of the reality of the noble profession they are entering. It doesn't stop the high fives and cheering of the small band of green handlers who are about to embark on a career with a built-in best friend.

★ ★ ★ 19 ★ ★ ★

DOG SCHOOL

It takes about five weeks longer to create a standard-issue dual-purpose military working dog than it does to graduate a handler. During this time, dog school instructors teach dogs fundamental obedience, detection, and patrol work. In the end, the dog will have a set of basic skills that can be built upon when he is assigned to a home base, where the dog will expand on the previous training.

Air Force Technical Sergeant Jason Barken, a master trainer and training team leader at Lackland, likens dog school to an assembly line. With eighteen to twenty-two dogs per team of trainers, and nine or ten teams of trainers at a time, some two hundred dogs can be going through training here, albeit at different stages of dog school. They're staggered so not all dogs end up in one place at one time.

Each team is made up of five to seven trainers, including a "red patch," or training supervisor. The red patches wear a red triangular-shaped patch on their tan overalls, which distinguishes them from all the other trainers wearing tan overalls on the team. When a team gets a trailer of dogs, they divvy them up. So for a typical trailer of eighteen dogs and a six-trainer team that will teach them the ropes, each trainer ends up with three.

While many dogs will already have some familiarity with bite training because the Department of Defense won't buy them if they don't have a decent bite, many don't know even the most elemental obedience. Most don't even know the command for "sit" or "lie down." And if they do, it may well be in Dutch or German.

Dogs go through detection training first. They'll learn eight explosives scents here (or a variety of narcotic scents), starting out in much the same fashion they did when they were chosen for this work from the vendors. Only this time instead of vanilla or licorice, trainers use real commercial explosives.

A dog may have a slight change of behavior when he smells a new scent like potassium chlorate—kind of like a "Whoa, that was weird! Let me give that an extra sniff" reaction. It can be very subtle. Sometimes it's just a little extra time spent on a scent. When the dog has clearly detected the odor, a trainer "pays on sniff" by throwing a Kong over the dog's head so it lands on the scent. It seems to the dog like it's not the trainer who pays him, but the scent.

That dogs can believe the scent of potassium chlorate magically creates a bouncing Kong is just one of those things that makes them lovable. The trainer doing the high-pitched happy cheerleading for the dog's deed might seem a little odd to the dog at first. One wonders if the dog thinks the handler is just as happy to see the Kong appear from the explosive as the dog himself is.

The reason for the ball coming from the odor and not from a trainer at this early stage is that the dog shouldn't always be looking to the trainer to see if he's on the right track. A dog can't have this kind of dependence in theater, since handlers have no idea where

IEDs may be. Looking for approval or reward in a wartime situation can lead to a dog stepping onto an IED instead of detecting it first.

After a while, when a dog detects the scent, he'll stare at it, which of course leads to the reward. Trainers then introduce the "sit" command when a dog sniffs an odor, because it's important that dogs don't keep wandering around once they've detected something, and because sitting makes it clear that the dog isn't just staring at a passing beetle. The technique where a dog sits and stares at an odor is known as deferred final response. Some dogs may lie down instead if the odor source is low or it's under something like a car.

Once a dog learns the technique for one scent, other scents can be fairly quick to follow. It's as if a lightbulb goes off: "Ah, here's a new, weird, unnatural, potent scent. Let's see if a Kong comes out of it!" After a while, the Kong doesn't even have to be used in this manner anymore, but it's inevitably part of the reward. The scents that dogs learn to detect at the 341st are just the start of a bouquet of narcotic or explosives scents they'll be able to uncover. Many more will be added as they continue their training at their home bases and beyond.

The detection portion of dog school takes about sixty days. In order to certify as a detection dog, drug dogs need to have 90 percent accuracy. Explosives dogs must have 95 percent, missing a maximum of one out of the twenty aids.

Then it's on to the patrol section of schooling. This starts with basic obedience, then ramps up to an obstacle course, with tunnels, a jump, stairs, and other structures similar to what dogs might encounter during a mission. Labradors and other dogs destined for a single-purpose career stop training here.

The shepherds and Malinois move on to the next phase of the dog school syllabus: the bite. Most dual-purpose dogs these days seldom need to use their bite skills in real life. But the deterrent factor may be part of the reason the dogs so rarely have to go into bite mode. Most people will back off when they see these dogs, or when the barking begins.

The dual-purpose dogs the Department of Defense purchases are already trained to bite, so the bite work is finessed and taken to the next level at Lackland. The dogs generally know how to run and attack a decoy's arm that's protected by a bite sleeve. It is deeply satisfying for a dog to chomp into it; in fact, the bite is the reward— no Kong needed.

But what about stopping someone who's running away? The dogs here work on an exercise called a field interview, where the handler is questioning a "bad guy," maybe frisking him. The decoy in this scenario is often clad in full-body protective gear, known affectionately as a marshmallow suit. It makes him look rather like the Michelin Man wearing a dark-colored coverall with thick fabric. The wearer's head is usually the only part that's not protected.

The dog stands guard. The person bolts. The handler shouts for him to stop, but he doesn't. Meanwhile the dog is completely at attention, ears forward, body stiff, tail rigid, eyes focused. The decoy is like a giant rabbit, and to a dog with a strong prey, hunt, or play drive, it's one of the most fun games there is.

(In case you ever get apprehended by a MWD or any law-enforcement canine, you might like to note that these dogs tend to bite the part of you that's moving the most. When you're sprawled out on the ground after a dog knocks you down, consider waving a white flag. And don't think about playing dead. The dog will liven you up very quickly.)

"Git him!" the trainer exhorts. Music to a dog's ears. The dog gallops to his quarry and grabs whatever body part is convenient. The force often knocks down the decoy. Whether the decoy remains standing or gets sent to the ground, a well-trained dog will bite and hang on until the trainer calls him off. Most dogs don't want to give up the bite. Some release immediately, others grab and shake until more firmly commanded—or even physically pried off. With more training, the release comes more quickly.

And what happens if, during the initial pursuit, the "bad guy" gives up and stops running? The dog needs to be able to stop in his tracks and resist every urge to finish the pursuit and bite the crap out of him until told to stop. This is called a standoff. The handler or trainer yells, "*Out,*" very loudly, and the dog is supposed to stop in his tracks and stand guard next to the suspect. The dog learns how to escort the suspect away, heeling close at his side. If the person makes a move to escape, the dog can grab him if the handler doesn't get to him first.

I've watched this type of dramatic exercise at a few different military bases, with the big padded man or woman flouting the law and running away. It made me wonder if dogs think that all bad guys are obese. The message seems to be "Great big person runs away, I get to bite." I've been assured that this isn't the case. It's the chase that kicks in a dog's instincts, not the size of the person. In fact, as a dog gets more advanced, there's special protective gear that's a lot less bulky than the marshmallow suit. It doesn't protect as well, so it's not used that much. But it helps make the scenario more realistic.

My question about bite-protection gear wasn't entirely unfounded, as it turned out. Over lunch at Chili's, Air Force Technical Sergeant Joe Null, the noncommissioned officer in charge of military working dog logistics, told me that there are some dogs who are so used to an obvious padded target—like a bite sleeve or full-body gear—that they're flummoxed when these are absent.

He pointed me to a grainy video on YouTube that shows what appears to be a real-life situation, taken from a helicopter camera that doesn't have the world's best zoom, of a police dog chasing a suspect. But as the dog gets ready to take down the man, you can see by the dog's body language that he's a little confused. Null says the dog is wondering, "Where's the bite sleeve? Where's the padding?" He passes the man by, slows his pace, and for the remainder of the short video, man and dog weave around each other along the road, the dog now looking like he's merrily cantering around—no longer an aggressor but more a happy cartoon character. When the music shifts from a dramatic chase riff to the Looney Tunes theme, it fits perfectly.

"The moral for handlers," says Null. "Don't let this happen to you."

But it's easy to see why some dogs are motivated by the sight and scent of a good bite sleeve—a big, thick, almost castlike arm protector. Everywhere I went at Lackland's patrol area, dogs with heads held high and tails wagging hard paraded around with what looked like giant, stiff arms. After certain types of exercises—like finding a bad guy behind a closed door in a barren building with many doors—dogs would get the sleeve as a reward for about a minute, and they'd beam as they toted around the biggest and most outlandish "bones" ever. It's no wonder the dog in the video was holding out for his. (Another theory about that dog is that he didn't want to hurt the man. He probably learned that handlers are not happy when you bite into a body part that's not protected.)

What starts as a fun game propelled by a dog's play, prey, and hunt drives develops over months and even years into a drive to defend and protect. "The goal is to develop the ultimate working dog that will defend itself and its pack members under any condition," Arod says. If a handler is wounded and unable to speak, the dog won't just stand there waiting for the command. He'll go into full protection mode.

The trainers at Lackland plant the seeds of this drive. They teach a dog to attack when the "bad guy" starts fighting, or even when a suspect raises his arm while being questioned in a mock field interview.

Not all dogs will make it through this part of dog school. Patrol is not for everyone. Just as Ferdinand the fictional bull preferred to just sit and sniff the flowers, some tough-looking military working dogs really don't want to attack people. There are softies in the dog world, and no matter what you do, they're not going to be reliable aggressors. "They just want to be your friend," says Null.

The military knows this, which is why dogs certify in detection work first. These dogs can be perfectly good sniffer dogs, and they have the bonus feature of looking like they could eat you for lunch, even if they'd rather just come over for a good ear rub.

★ ★ ★ 20 ★ ★ ★

I TRY NOT TO NOTICE THE BLOOD

I've been watching bite-training work at Lackland for much of the morning when I meet up with Navy Master-at-Arms First Class Ekali Brooks. He's training new students at the handler course on the basics of "catching" a dog.

When you catch a dog, the dog—generally a German shepherd or a Belgian Malinois—careens toward you at top speed, intent on biting into the part of your body that's easiest to access and that's moving the most. This can be rather dangerous, so you wear a bite sleeve. If you catch a dog right, you won't be hurt. Mess up, and you might know what a few hundred psi of dog bite feels like.

Brooks explains that as the dog runs at you, the sleeve needs to be a few inches away from your body so there's a cushion when the impact occurs. More experienced handlers and trainers can be running away from the dog and turn at the last second for the dog to bite into the sleeve. New students just stand there facing the dog, knees bent, ready to absorb the impact. In either case, as the dog runs toward you, you want to agitate the sleeve, shaking your arm so the dog is attracted to the sleeve and not to any of the many unprotected parts of the body.

As I watch dogs fly by on the field of dry grass on this scorching Texas summer day, I realize a lot of things can go wrong if you don't do this decoy business right. (Brooks tells me that "decoy" is a more appropriate term for what I'd been calling the "dog catcher" or once even, carelessly, the "victim.") Besides the scars so many handlers and trainers bear, Brooks says these men and women are notorious for having shoulder problems.

Then he asks someone nearby a question: "You want to catch a dog?"

I look around for the decoy candidate he's talking to, but there's no one else close enough to hear that question.

"You want to try it?"

Oh God, the man is looking at *me*. And he's smiling in that benevolent "here is a gift I know you will love" kind of way. How can I say no?

"Sure, that'd be great!" Suddenly the hot day feels much warmer.

Brooks calls over a husky student wearing army camouflage and asks for his sleeve. It looks like the arm of the Tin Man from *The Wizard of Oz*, only with a jute fiber cover over hard plastic. It's a Gappay brand—one of the best, Arod would later tell me—and starts at the shoulder, bends ninety degrees at the elbow, and ends well past the hand, which is sealed off in case of overly enthusiastic dogs.

Brooks hands it to me, and I try not to notice that there's blood on the outside. The jute should be a nice haylike color. And it mostly is. But there's one area that's the color and demeanor of the piece of absorbent material that's on the bottom of a package of hamburger meat. I didn't want to ask what happened. Better not to know right now.

(I later learn that the blood is from the friction of a dog's gums against the jute, not from a handler mishap. It's uncommon that a dog bites in such a way that the gums scrape and bleed, but the sleeve I was wearing was pretty tattered and had clearly caught hundreds of dogs, and rubbed at least one dog's gums the wrong way.)

I slip my arm into the thing. Inside there's foam cushioning and a bar of protective steel running the length of it. The cushioning has a sticky, grungy, spongy wetness from the sweat of the handlers who've been practicing this morning. Outside, the jute is shredded and damp from the saliva of dogs with great big canine teeth and an even bigger prey drive. The dog I'm about to catch—a smaller, older Belgian Malinois named Laika H267—eyes me and my giant arm from afar. She looks like she wants a piece of me. I tuck away any thoughts of arms as hamburger meat and get my instructions from Brooks.

He is confident and calm in manner and has done this for years. He has an enthusiasm about working with dogs that's conveniently contagious. "They actually pay us to work with dogs like this! There aren't too many people who like what they do, and I love what I do. It doesn't get any better than working with these dogs."

My arm is in good hands.

I'm positioned, knees slightly bent, arm a few inches from torso. Bring on the Malinois!

Then I remember the missing ear.

It's earlier that same morning, around 6:30 A.M., not too warm just yet for the birds in a pleasant grove of trees to pack up their songs for the day. Shade is a precious commodity at Lackland, and about ten new handler course students are starting their day under the trees, bonding with the dogs. They've been assigned these dogs for a few weeks now, and some are really getting attached.

The students smooth their hands down their dogs' coats repeatedly, and they talk to them. It's a practice called rapport work. The touch and closeness helps establish the students as people the dogs should care about. And it helps the students get to know their dogs as well. Some dogs don't even seem to notice all the attention and spend the time barking at another dog or running back and forth as far as their leash will allow. But most dogs revel in it.

I approach a navy student handler whose dog is standing still, eyes slightly shut, as he enjoys the military's version of a dog massage. The dog is a large shepherd with bushy fur around his ears. His real name is Hugo P128, but Navy Master-at-Arms Seaman Glenn Patton calls him Chewbacca because of the dog's similarity to the hirsute *Star Wars* character. Patton beams as he strokes his dog.

"Oh, I love him. I'd take him home if I could," he tells me when I ask how they're getting on. As we talk about his lifelong love for dogs, and how he has dreamed of being a military dog handler for years, he turns his head slightly to the left, and I notice that the upper third of his right ear is missing.

The top edge of what's left of the ear is jagged and red, almost like someone or something recently bit it off. This turns out to be an accurate assessment. He explains, after some coaxing, that another dog had bolted away from his handler the previous week and tried to attack Hugo. Patton came between, and the aggressor bit into his ear and ripped it off.

I found out later that a group of handlers and instructors searched for the ear in the vicinity of the attack for a long time and couldn't find it. In an effort to leave no stone unturned, the perpetrator dog was brought to the vet and given an emetic to induce vomiting. But when he threw up, there was no ear.

Patton says the mishap hasn't discouraged him from his calling. "In a weird way, it's made me love it even more. It shows me that my love for the program is as deep as I thought it would be. It doesn't bother me what happened. I just keep loving working with dogs and can't believe my good luck that I'm here."

"Get her!"

Laika lunges toward me. I start shaking my giant, sleeved arm at the Malinois as instructed, so she'll be attracted to that part of my body and not (oh, just for instance) my ear. As she runs toward me, Brooks tells me to freeze. I stop moving so she'll get a good bite on the targeted body part.

Laika is on a long leash just in case, but the impact is strong. She sends me reeling back a step, and the sleeve crashes into my body. She starts tearing at the sleeve, and as I agitate it again she digs in, front paws pushing against my stomach and then my thigh for more leverage. Her bite is steady and strong. The power of this dog's mouth is awesome. Without the sleeve, I'd be a bloody mess.

Having Laika on my arm starts to be almost fun. Brooks tells me I can growl at her, so I do and she digs in harder. Then he tells me they always praise a dog, so I tell her what a good girl she is before I realize that as the bad guy I'm probably not the one who is supposed to praise her. But she continues biting just as hard, unfazed by my complimentary words, and perhaps a little concerned about my apparent mood swings. Then Brooks comes over and gives Laika a friendly "atta girl" pat.

"Decoy, stop resisting!" he shouts to me, and I stop moving my arm. "Out!" he calls to the dog. Laika stops biting, but on the way down, quickly butts my torso with her nose. "Sit!" She sits. "Stay." I back away several steps when Brooks tells me to. Laika trots off with her handler, and as she does, she turns around and looks at me with what could only be described as a "Wait till next time" expression.

★ ★ ★ 21 ★ ★ ★

REWARD-BASED TRAINING, MOSTLY

Laika's reward—aka "pay"—was twofold: biting my arm, and the praise from Brooks. If she wanted a piece of me again, maybe it was only because dogs love the rewards of the job.

I came to Lackland wondering what style of training would be used on the dogs. These are strong dogs with great fortitude and will. I expected to witness some manhandling but hoped there would be nothing too brutal.

So I was surprised to see that training here is mostly about positive reinforcement. Dogs who did well got their rewards and heaps of happy praise. In detection work, failure to notice a scent just meant no reward. There was no yelling, no dragging the dog over and shoving his nose in the odor. The patrol side was only slightly different. Praise and Kongs and bite sleeves flew all around, but if a dog didn't listen to a command during bite work—for instance, if he didn't stop when a trainer shouted *"Out!"*—he'd get a quick, light jerk on his choke chain, and he'd be walked back to start the exercise again.

"It's much more fun, much more rewarding, less inhibiting

than other training methods," says Arod. "Since you don't use compulsion or what would be considered traditional punishment, it doesn't affect the softer dogs badly."

Months after my visits to Lackland, I ran into dog trainer Victoria Stillwell at the American Humane Association Hero Dog Awards in Beverly Hills. She has drawn a tremendous audience by espousing positive training only. We got to talking, and I thought she'd be pretty happy with the positive training I generally saw wherever I went for the book research. But she said she still thinks there's room for improvement in military working dog training. "You can train even really aggressive dogs in a positive manner. You don't need to jerk a collar. Dogs should not have to have choke collars at all."

Doc Hilliard, who has been instrumental in developing training techniques for the dog school, says that patrol can be done without any sort of correction for some special dogs, "but takes a lot of time. We don't have this kind of time, and the dogs we get are not prepared for pure positive training."

In my travels to military dog training areas, I have never seen anything more than a collar jerk. Even when a dog ran hundreds of yards away from his handler during off-leash exercises in the Arizona desert, he did not get chastised when the handler and an instructor found him. In fact, he got extra care. "Get him water. Take his temperature. Put him in the trailer so he has some AC." It was no act put on because a reporter was there. You could tell this was just protocol. I was amazed at the restraint. Even I might have had a few words with Jake had he made me run a few hundred yards in 112-degree weather.

Military working dog training has changed dramatically in the last twenty years, according to Doc Hilliard. As he explains it, traditional methods used to involve compelling a dog to perform obedience by using corrections, normally by jerking or by tightening a chain choke collar. The reward was understood to be release from this pressure, combined with petting and praise. While the praise was positive, the system was fundamentally "compulsive" in outlook because the dog was not given any choices; he was compelled to do as the trainer demanded.

The system worked, but sometimes produced dogs who feared their trainers and did not like work. These days, the dog program is moving toward more "inducive" systems of training, in which training is broken into three stages. In the first stage the dog is taught what commands mean by using a reward like a Kong or a ball. This reward is used to "lure" the animal into a correct position (for example, lying down) and then the dog is rewarded. If the dog does not carry out the command, there is no penalty other than simply not giving the dog the reward. In the second phase, trainers layer on some physical correction such as a soft pop on the leash. They teach the dog that this pop on the leash is associated, for instance, with breaking the down position before permission from the handler. This is how a dog comes to understand that certain actions are associated with collar pressure and certain others with lack of collar pressure.

In the final phase, the dog learns that he must carry out commands, no matter what the situation or how many distractions. In this phase, sharper collar corrections are used, and the dog is not given the option to do as he wishes. However, throughout all three phases, even the last, rewards such as a toy are still given to the dog when he performs correctly. As a result, trainers produce a dog who understands his work clearly, understands that corrections will be associated with mistakes or disobedience, but fundamentally likes his work because he has a clear understanding of what is expected—and because he often receives rewards.

That's not to say harsher methods are never used, at least once the dogs are beyond boot camp level. There are "harder," very aggressive dogs for whom I'm told nothing else has worked. The trick, say the handlers, is to remain calm and in control while getting the dog's attention via a little "ass whupping." A dog who's not backing off an attack on another dog or handler can be thrown on his back and slapped (not hard) on his face, for instance, and no other handlers are likely to cry foul. The idea is not to hurt the dog, but to let him know in no uncertain terms that this behavior will not be tolerated.

But every so often, a handler will go too far. These seem to be blissfully rare events, but they're disturbing nonetheless. An out-of-control handler may kick or punch a dog, pick him up high and slam him hard to the ground, use a cattle prod, or even helicopter a dog. (The latter, unfortunately, sounds like what it is, with spinning and fear involved. It can end with a slam to the ground if the handler has really lost it.)

These methods are not only highly discouraged, an individual can be brought up on Uniform Code of Military Justice charges for abusing a dog. The consequences can range from being given extra work to loss of rank or even dog-handler status, or full court-martial that could result in a felony conviction. Marine Captain John "Brandon" Bowe says most cases never go to court-martial but are taken care of in a process called nonjudicial punishment (NJP). "Dog handlers tend to be a cut above, so NJP usually solves matters."

Justice can come from unexpected places. It is not unheard of for instructors or other handlers to mete out quid pro quo punishment. Kick a dog hard in the belly when he's already on his back, for instance, and don't be surprised when what goes around comes around.

I heard about a situation that didn't involve abuse, but accidental neglect. A handler forgot his dog in the dog trailer on a hot summer day. The AC wasn't on, because the dogs were all supposed to be out of the trailer. The dog could have died but was found in time. So he would never forget his dog again, the handler was tied up, shoved in a kennel, and driven out to the training area. He stayed there for a few hours. There are no reports of him forgetting another dog.

With the way that dogs have become a deeply integral part of our families and our lives in the last couple of decades, it's natural to think that the military's stand on positive reinforcement training is a recent development—one that adheres to philosophies like the following, from a book about training war dogs:

> The highest qualities of mind—love and duty—have to be appealed to and cultivated. . . . The whole training is based on appeal. To this end the dog is gently taught to associate everything pleasant with its working hours. Under no circumstances whatever must it be roughly handled or roughly spoken to. If it makes a mistake, or is slack in its work when being trained, it is never chastised, but is merely shown how to do it over again.

If any of the men under instruction are observed to display roughness or lack of sympathy with the dogs, they should be instantly dismissed, as a promising young dog could easily be thrown back in his training, or even spoiled altogether, by sharp handling. . . . No whips should exist in the training school and are never necessary; gentle, steady routine work is the right method of impressing the dog's intelligence, and kindly encouragement and caresses will meet its desire to understand, better than coercive measures or rebukes.

Modern thinking, to be sure. Only the author, Lieutenant Colonel Edwin H. Richardson, founder of the British War Dog School, wrote it in 1920. It's from his book *British War Dogs: Their Training and Psychology*, which—together with his articles and influence during both World War I and II—helped set the stage for how the U.S. would train war dogs when this country finally got our program going during World War II.

Richardson believed that positive reinforcement was the only way to successfully train a dog, that in the end you had to appeal to a dog's good nature and desire to please. War-dog historian Michael Lemish says that the military followed this doctrine of positive reinforcement and never supported brutality or harsh treatment. But it hasn't all been ear scratches and rubber balls for soldier dogs. For instance, mine-detecting dogs in World War II were frequently trained using electric shock collars.

And one form of training for sentry dogs in Vietnam sounds pretty crazy. It was called the agitation method and is described as "getting the dog excited about attacking his prey. Usually a small branch would be used and whacked across his backside to make the dog even more excited about going after his prey. It was not punishment."

Those were some of the few real sticks officially used. These days, carrots are everything.

A handler told me about the first bomb dog he had. The dog was a veteran and knew exactly what was expected of him. "He'd be like, 'Get my Kong ready and get set to praise me up, and I'll go find a bomb for you.' When you think of what this rubber toy inspires, it's just incredible."

The training and handling of military working dogs today just wouldn't be the same without the Kong. It was, fittingly, a retired police dog named Fritz who inspired the creation of this hard rubber toy. Back in the mid-1970s, the German shepherd was always chewing rocks, cans, anything hard he could get his mouth around. It frustrated his owner, Joe Markham, to no end. One day, as Markham was doing some repairs to his 1967 Volkswagen van, Fritz started chewing rocks again. To distract him, Markham threw Fritz various van parts he was through with. The dog took no interest in the radiator hoses and other bits flying toward him, until Markham tossed a hard rubber suspension part to his dog. Fritz went mad for it.

Markham knew he was on to something. He finessed a design and found a rubber manufacturing plant near his Colorado home. After seeing the prototype, his business partner said it looked like an earplug for King Kong, and a name was born. Kongs are still made in Colorado, of a proprietary superstrong rubber. They dominate the dog-toy market.

Kongs are ubiquitous in the military working dog world. You'll find Kongs at every military kennel and, really, anyplace in the world where there are U.S. military dogs. Lackland ordered nearly one thousand Kong toys in 2010, just for the dog school and handler course. Kongs even show up all over Afghanistan now, thanks to the presence of working dogs there. A Kong representative says the company donates thousands of Kongs annually to military dog facilities and handlers.

Kong is not one toy but actually a line of hard rubber dog toys. The most popular Kongs in the military are red or black, with what looks like three balls of different sizes fused together in a snowmanlike configuration. They're hollow inside, and many civilians like to stuff treats into them to keep their dogs occupied with getting them out.

But in the military, Kongs are not used in this manner. They're bouncy rewards that supplement the dog's primary reward of pleasing the handler. (Some trainers say that the reverse is true—that handlers are secondary rewards to Kongs and other toys. It likely depends on the dog and handler.) Kongs gratify a dog's prey and play drives. Toss a Kong on the ground, and it doesn't bounce true, as a tennis ball does. (Military dogs also get tennis balls as rewards. Even a glove will do in a pinch.) Its odd shape causes the Kong to bounce and skip erratically, much like a fleeing rabbit or other prey. Dogs chase, catch, and experience what's apparently the unparalleled feeling of the toy/prey in their mouths.

"To the dog with a high prey drive, the Kong is a million-dollar paycheck. You throw it and it's run, chase, bite! They can't help themselves," says Gunnery Sergeant Kristopher Knight. But there are soldier dogs whose prey drive isn't so strong. Kongs or praise or even food rewards may not be enough pay for them to do their jobs well. These dogs may certify at dog school and even do passably well at their home bases. But when they deploy to a place like Afghanistan, the motivation to sniff for IEDs can be the sole factor that separates life and death—for the dogs, their handlers, and anyone nearby.

Gunfire, mortar blasts, IED explosions, and intense heat are part of the canvas of extreme conditions troops and dogs have to deal with in that war-ravaged country. Even dogs with fine prey drives can have difficulty functioning well once they deploy to this foreign, oft-hostile setting.

Fortunately, soldier dogs and handlers have a Stateside location where they go to prepare for the rigors of deploying to this kind of environment. If you were blindfolded and taken there, you could easily think you were already deployed.

PART THREE

★ ★ ★

THE DOG TRAINER
AND THE SCIENTISTS

★ ★ ★ 22 ★ ★ ★

AFGHANISTAN, USA

When you walk by an empty dog trailer, it's supposed to be silent. And when Marine Gunnery Sergeant Kristopher Knight—known to his commanding officer, Captain John "Brandon" Bowe, as "the smartest and most amazing man on the planet to train dogs"—passes within two feet of a trailer's empty kennels on a 110-degree August afternoon at the Yuma Proving Ground, it is indeed mute. But when I walk past it a few seconds later, I'm surprised when a series of hefty barks fly out of a lone dog, Rocky P506. He's waiting in semi air-conditioned comfort while the rest of his class tracks faux bad guys in the distance. He is there as backup, in case any of the dogs are too spooked to track well after a hair-raising helicopter ride that was part of the day's training. He won't stop barking at me, even when I'm twenty feet away.

"Hey, Gunny, why didn't that dog bark at *you*?" I ask.

"Heh heh," he answers and we walk on.

We return about an hour later after watching the dog's colleagues at work, and Gunny passes by the trailer. Once again, silence. As soon as I get within a few feet, a deep *RAW RAW RAW* staccatos at me.

"Gunny, why is he only barking at *me*?" Dogs always like me. What's up with this one?

"Could be any number of factors, even something like you're not in a uniform. He's used to people in uniform," he explains.

The barking continues and Gunny Knight walks toward the trailer. "Watch this. You can breathe on him and calm him down." He goes up to the German shepherd, who is still barking in my direction behind the metal bars of his kennel. Gunny blows a stream of air gently on his head, and the dog almost instantaneously quiets down and sits.

Bowe told me that Gunny has a way with dogs that no one else has. "He talks dog. That's the thing about Gunny Knight. He speaks their language. He speaks dog slang. He speaks dog English. He speaks dog Ebonics. No matter what language, he knows how to read dogs, talk dogs, train dogs, and I've never seen in all my years in the Marine Corps—and that's going on twenty—anyone who can work with dogs like him."

I get closer to look at this transformed canine, in awe of what Gunny has done. Suddenly Rocky starts in at me again.

"Go ahead, breathe on him," Gunny instructs. "Let him smell that you are calm and can control him, you are in charge."

I conjure up the words "I'm the calm boss" in my brain, and I exhale gently on Rocky's head. It doesn't work. I realize that while I'm calm, I'm not feeling like the boss, just making up the words. So I channel Gunny Knight as my persona. No words this time, just a feeling—a benevolent authority; I am momentarily muscle-bound, with a big cocky grin. I exhale, briefly becoming Gunny Knight, breathing Gunny Knight vibes onto Rocky's head.

Rocky suddenly stops. He sits and looks at me, mouth slightly open, seeming almost relaxed. He stays like that even as I walk away with Gunny.

What just happened?

Gunny tells me that he uses this technique to calm down dogs and let them smell the chemical cocktail that is uniquely him. "By doing so, the dog is able to determine multiple factors about me—confidence, fear, threatening behaviors, trust, calm nature, etc."

I later ran the incident by canine cognition expert Alexandra Horowitz. I thought she'd know exactly what magic Gunny had worked. But somewhat surprisingly, she said that it's common wisdom in dog circles that blowing on a dog's face is an aggressive action. "I could conjecture that a dog who is blown on might stop being restless, but not necessarily because they feel calm. They might feel alarmed, too. I would have to see the rest of the dog's behavior and posture in context to get a read on this marine's dogs."

If Horowitz had been dealing with a standard military dog trainer, her desire to observe and understand the situation might have paid off with scientifically based insights drawn from other similar observations. But there is nothing standard about Gunny Knight.

And there's nothing terribly ordinary about the predeployment course for dogs and handlers he runs in this arid corner of Arizona bordering Mexico and California. I learned this one dark June morning, at 4:30 A.M., when I first set foot on the Yuma Proving Ground.

THE PROVING GROUND

A full moon hovers over rows of open-air kennels, where the cacophony of barking punctuates the warm predawn desert air. Sixteen handlers in camo greet their excited dogs and leash them up for their morning constitutionals. Two klicks away, down a dusty road, an ammo recovery team sets out explosives in Taliban fashion, hiding them, covering them with dirt and pebbles, making them look just like any other part of the terrain.

Gunny Knight calls over to me and has me hop into his Isuzu VehiCROSS—one of only four thousand that were ever sold in the U.S. over several years, he will tell you.

We drive to a place called Site 2. As we're driving, the sun climbs over the horizon, casting new light on what was only a milky visage moments ago. Flat, dry, unforgiving Sonoran Desert terrain spreads out for miles in every direction, with low, jagged mountains fringing the desolate landscape. You would not want to be lost here.

I'm thinking about how much it looks like images I've seen of parts of Afghanistan, when I spot people falling out of the sky. They're dangling from parachutes, twenty of them, getting almost alarmingly close to us. I'm fascinated. They're clearly Special Ops guys of some form—who knows, maybe even related to Cairo's people. My excitement is lost on Gunny. He scoffs. "Clowns. When's the last time anyone ever parachuted into combat?"

We drive around for awhile so I can get the lay of the land, and by the time we arrive at our destination, eight handlers are finishing a long run. It's already eighty-three degrees. Some are sweating and red, others (marines, mostly) look like they just stepped out of a cool cafe. Then it's military push-up time. As they wrap up PT, the moon disappears, and the dogs who have been barking in their trailers come out and chug water from gallon jugs. It's now 6 A.M. and time to start the day.

Military working dog handlers deploying to work outside the wire are supposed to go through rigorous predeployment training, generally at a course designed to prepare them and their dogs for the grueling demands of war. There's a canine team predeployment course at Creech Air Force Base in Nevada and one at Fort Dix in New Jersey.

But the course that every handler and instructor I talked with across all four services says is *the* course to attend is the Inter-Service Advanced Skills K-9 (IASK) Course, here at the Yuma Proving Ground. It is the only advanced course among the three, and it focuses entirely on matters essential to dog teams. In addition, it's the only course that accepts dog handlers from all four services. Those who have gone through this Marine Corps–run program rave about the training, despite its rigors: "No other course compares." "It'll save your life, and maybe a lot of other lives." "A killer, but the best training in the entire military." "Should be mandatory for every handler deploying." "Gunny Knight knows his shit like no one else."

The course takes advantage of its location, and at thirteen hundred square miles, it is one of the largest military installations in the world. YPG is known for testing munitions systems and weapons, military vehicles, and manned and unmanned aviation systems. In addition, some thirty-six thousand parachute drops take place annually here—apparently much to Gunny Knight's annoyance. As the day goes on, and the sky divers drop from planes like tiny bursts of rain, there is always a new name. This time it's "Damned glory children!" You get the impression that these parachutists are in the same category as mosquitoes to this man. Or maybe it goes deeper than that.

The terrain and the climate make the Yuma Proving Ground a popular training area for all kinds of units that will be deploying. The IASK course adds some authentic man-made touches, with a mock "Middle East" village; it's home to a mosque, mud and concrete buildings, and a small marketplace. At Site 2 there's a two-story compound surrounded by walls—a small and simpler version of Bin Laden's final manse. And because this is a test facility, the course gets munitions and ordnance no other military working dog courses can.

During the course, which runs for nineteen days, dogs and handlers take part in realistic raids, night operations, and route-clearance exercises. The machines that simulate ammo, IED, and mortar blasts are deafening, the humps are long and arduous, and the heat is stultifying. "A lot of dogs who are good at their home station in a cooler area come here and shit the bed. Like 'Sweet Jesus, I can't feel my balls and I can't breathe by 11 A.M.!'

"But if you have not subjected your dog to this terrain, to this temperature, you really don't know how he's going to perform. You don't know how you're going to do, either," Gunny says as he watches a navy handler struggle to put on his pack.

One of the most valuable parts of the course is the exposure to homemade explosives (HMEs). It's estimated that HMEs account for 90 percent of the explosives being used in Afghanistan right now. It's so important that dogs get imprinted with these scents that Gunny Knight even offers a special mini-course that handlers can come here for.

Before Corporal Max Donahue and his dog, Fenji, deployed to Afghanistan, they took the HME course. They did very well here, and Donahue spread the word to other marine handlers that the HME course was not to be missed. "It's going to save you, your dog, and all those guys following you," he would tell them.

He got it straight from Gunny Knight. "If your dog has never been subject to HMEs, what's the point of even going to Afghanistan? It's like going to combat with a rifle and no ammo." You can't expect a dog to find something he was never trained to find. Ammonium nitrate? It might as well be a bowl of grapes to your dog, because if he's never been rewarded for locating it and responding to it, why would he place any value on it?

When Master Chief Scott Thompson headed dog operations in Afghanistan from 2010 to mid-2011, he was in frequent communication with Gunny Knight, letting him know the most recent Taliban trends in explosives and IED placement methods. Now it's pretty much the handlers doing it. They hear what to watch out for pretty fast from other handlers over there. They tell Gunny and his staff, and they're on it. Handlers who have been through this course say they were very well prepared for the Taliban's latest tricks.

Seven A.M. and Air Force Technical Sergeant Gwendolyn Dodd is giving the first handler of the day his final instructions. As she talks to him, the mortar and ammo simulators are already going off around the compound. Dodd and the handler and his dog are at the back end and have to enter the compound area by crawling through a long, dusty tunnel. "Ready?" she asks, and then sees the handler's canine partner. The dog is busy doing a leg lift on a solo scrap of plant life. It's a moment that makes you see the dog for what he is: Not a warrior. Just a dog like yours or mine. "Go ahead, boy!" he tells his dog enthusiastically when his dog has finished. The dog charges through. Dodd and the dog's handler follow.

Gunny and I meet them at the edge of the compound. During the next two hours, we will see two more handlers go through the same raid exercise. Wearing full combat gear, rifles poised, they walk next to an outer compound wall, carefully watching around them for snipers and other dangers, and observing their dogs. They negotiate corners, sometimes well, sometimes badly. One handler walks around a corner in front of his dog, and if this were the real deal, he'd have set off several IEDs. But the course's chief instructor, Marine Staff Sergeant Kenny Porras, stops him and reminds him that the dog has to go first. So the handler lets the dog go first, and the German shepherd immediately lies down, tail wagging, looking earnestly at what seems to be plain gravel and dirt, just like everything around it. It isn't until Knight brushes away some dust and gravel that I see the IEDs (which don't have fuses or detonators, so are safe) that lay underneath.

Once inside the compound, there are rooms to clear, stairs to negotiate. The mortar and ammo simulators go off nonstop nearby, and the heat in the plywood bowels of the compound gets more suffocating as the morning wears on. The dogs, though, are enthusiastic and don't seem to mind any of it. They find explosives in ceilings, behind boxes; they locate caches, and with every find, tails wag and they know they've done well and here comes the Kong and the whoop and the praise, and a minute later the party is over and it's off to search for more.

"There's a lot of dogs I wouldn't follow," says Gunny. "But if they make it through this course, I'd be right behind them downrange."

★ ★ ★ **24** ★ ★ ★

GUN-SHY

About 10 percent of teams that start the course don't grad-uate.

Skittish, fearful, gun-shy dogs or dogs who are very distractible or unfit do not make good soldier dogs. And sometimes handlers themselves are out of shape, they make too many excuses, or, Gunny points out, they cry too much. Gunny Knight and his team of instructors try to work with dogs and handlers who need extra help. He doesn't like cutting handlers.

"My biggest fear in life is failure. So I imagine how they feel when they fail. Even if it's one hundred percent the dog's fault, it's not a joyous time. But I can't let them get out there and have others following them, thinking they're safe because they're behind the dog.

"See this guy?" he says, nodding his chin toward a navy handler who is working with his dog to clear a dirt road of IEDs. "I'm bru-tally honest. If he was terrible I would tell him, 'You're terrible,' and we'd do something about it. I don't really care to hear that this kid got killed three months after he went to our course."

If you ask him (and you don't have to, because he will be sure to tell you in the course of any conversation, even about the weather), some handlers play war fighter, but don't fight the war. They do the minimum required explosives exercises and physical training at their home bases and don't work their dogs more than twenty minutes at one time. When they get to Knight's course, they have a hard time.

We walk up the road to the compound, where a dog is sniffing for IEDs in front of his handler as the blast simulators make it hard to hear anything unless it's shouted. It's an intense scene. You could imagine this is the real deal in Afghanistan, except the dog team would have a lot more troops following. Then the dog sees a rock and walks over to it with great interest. Has he found an explosive? He sniffs. Inspects. Sniffs some more. Then he lifts his leg and splashes the rock, and moves on.

Dogs have to do their business. But some are too distractible. It's merely annoying when Jake is marking something every two feet on a walk, but in the theater of war, it can be deadly. "If his dog's like, 'Whatever!' and goes and pees and poops everywhere and doesn't find anything, they're gonna be like, 'Go sit in a corner and color. We'll take this guy instead.' Then the other handler has an extra burden, and the team may be worked too much, which takes a toll on their accuracy as well. So the goal is for all dog teams going over to be strong and reliable."

On another visit to Yuma in August, we're watching a new group of handlers, again in full combat gear, despite the 110-degree temperatures. It's a little earlier in the course, and these handlers are getting their first taste of looking for pressure plates and other IEDs in this terrain. The devices have no explosive traces, so the exercise is for the handlers only, not the dogs. They need to be able to see the telltale signs that someone has been there: A little pattern of gravel that doesn't fit in with the rest of the terrain. A wire barely covered with dirt. A round piece of metal that looks like a large soda cap; is it different from the other bits of litter in the area?

Porras has instructed them to just look and not say anything about where faux IEDs might be until the end of the exercise. Oh, and don't step on anything suspicious. The handlers all mill around a small gravelly lot, looking down, walking slowly, cautiously. A couple of minutes in, Gunny shouts out to a handler.

"How ya feeling?"

"Pretty good."

"Are you feeling kind of light?"

"No."

"Well you should be, because you just stepped on that pressure plate two times! If this were Afghanistan, you'd be missing a few limbs by now." The handler laughs, slightly embarrassed. The gallows humor gets the point across. The handlers walk even more slowly and seriously, inspecting the ground for the most subtle signs.

After Porras briefs them on where the devices were hidden—a few were so stealth no one guessed—he has them walk their dogs in a big oval as ammo and mortar simulators blast noisily, and at unpredictable intervals, just ten feet away. They walk around a couple of times, and Gunny leans in and points to a German shepherd and a Belgian Malinois who are looking up at their handlers more than the others. "They're going to have problems in a minute." They look OK to me, but in a minute I see he has pegged them.

With every explosion, both dogs flinch low to the ground, as if someone were about to hit them. Or they tuck their tails and try to run. It's painful to watch. The other dogs, for the most part, don't even seem to notice the blasts. They trot with tails high or focus with tails relaxed. But these two are distressed. The handler of the Malinois tries to quickly comfort his dog after each blast.

Blast.

He pats his dog's flanks.

Blast.

"It's OK!" he tells his dog.

Gunny beckons the handler over and takes the dog's leash. He walks the dog a few more feet away from the blast simulators, and the dog sits and looks at him. He strokes the dog's head gently, bending down and looking calmly into his eyes, rubbing under his chin, then back over his ears. The dog looks up, already seeming a little more relaxed. Gunny walks him away from the blasts and then turns toward the sounds. As he does, he faces the dog, who sits and then jumps up and puts his paws on Gunny's chest. Gunny strokes him some more and then gently uses his knee to coerce the dog back to sitting.

They do this a few more times, getting closer to the simulators, only he doesn't let the dog jump up anymore. He just pets the dog when he sits, leaning close and looking into his eyes. There is something about his demeanor that says, "You're going to be fine. Don't pay these noises any attention. Trust me on this." He hands the leash back to the handler, who has been crouched, watching. As the handler walks away, his dog tries to pull back to Gunny, and then he turns two more times toward him until he's once again swallowed back up in the oval.

"You have to show the dog real confidence. When you're

confident, your dog sees and feels that, and he feels safe," Gunny explains.

The dog still flinches, but maybe not quite so much. A work in progress.

Blast.

The handler pats his dog's head again.

"Don't reinforce it! Ignore it!" Gunny shouts.

He explains that with his well-meaning comforting, the handler is actually conditioning the dog to think that these noises are frightening. "His feelings are dumping down the leash right onto his dog, and the dog goes, 'Yeah, I thought I was right about being scared.'"

Of course, the dog's instincts are right. Hell yes, those blasts could mean some nasty business. And letting a dog think otherwise is just fooling this creature who will try his hardest to do whatever you ask of him. But the reality is that these dogs are deploying. In war, what good does it do for the dog to know those sounds could mean tremendous pain, or death?

So with ammo exposure, the idea is this: The dog needs to believe the sounds are not associated with danger. When the dog hears the blasts and gunfire enough times, and if the sounds have never been associated with anything bad, even sensitive dogs will usually come to shrug off the blasts. In Gunnyspeak (he frequently talks from a dog's POV), the MWD thinks, "I've heard these sounds a thousand times and I've never been shot, so why should I care about one thousand and one? Hey, when I find things when these sounds are going off, I get my reward. This is kind of fun!"

Next up is the other fearful dog. This time it's going to be a game. Gunny gets the dog's Kong rope toy from the handler, takes over the leash, and runs away from the simulators with the dog. As a blast goes off, he gives the dog his reward. They go back and forth several times. He's trying to distract the dog from the blasts, so he signals to someone on his crew whenever he wants an explosion. He gives the dog his rope toy and the blast goes off. At first the dog lets it go. But after several times, he's hanging on to it more. He's still not happy about the noise, but there has been some improvement by the time Gunny gives the dog back. He says it's not an ideal way to train a dog. Working a dog a little farther from the noise and working him up to it slowly is better, as is not using a reward quite so frequently. But he couldn't stand there and watch without trying a little first aid.

Back in June I met a navy team that did not end up passing the course. "I could tell right away the dog did not have the drive," Gunny says. One morning, while the German shepherd (who shall remain nameless, because his handler understandably felt bad about not passing) was standing with his handler, Gunny went up to him in a semi-threatening manner, waving his hat at the dog as he quickly weaved toward him. The dog stood up slowly and gave a couple of noncommittal barks. Gunny tried to engage him again and got really close. If the dog wanted to, he could have lunged, and if Gunny had not been speedy, he could have ended up missing part of his face. He riled up the dog a little, and the dog made some effort to pull toward Gunny and barked with more attitude. But it wasn't the kind of response Gunny was looking for.

During the raid and other war scenarios, the dog had put in the effort, but in the end, he didn't have the drive to want his reward badly enough to perform as he needed to.

"The dog's like, 'None of this crap is worth it and all I want to do is sit in front of a sixty-five-year-old lady's fireplace and relax,'" says Gunny. The team will continue to work on building up drive and confidence back at home base.

★ ★ ★ **25** ★ ★ ★

SHEEPLE

One thing Gunny can't stand seeing is a team with a handler that's not a strong leader. There are those who argue that the alpha dog/beta dog model is archaic and based on outdated information. But you won't find many supporters of this argument in the military working dog world.

"Two betas don't make a right," says Gunny Knight. "Too often you've got a beta leader. Every successful team needs a strong alpha leader, and that has to be the handler, not the dog.

"You see all these people these days following everyone else. They don't think. They don't know how to lead. Even in the military. Too many people, they're like sheep. People are becoming sheeple. It's no way to be in life, and it's no way to be a handler.

"I am not a sheeple."

Gunny Knight does not need to tell me this. I realized he was not a sheeple from our first conversation. Arod had told me about the Yuma course, and I knew I had to see it in person. I went through the proper media channels. Two weeks later, I received a phone call from a public affairs officer telling me they were processing my request, that it might take a little time, but that they'd do their best.

A couple of days later I got a call from a man with a booming voice. He introduced himself as Gunnery Sergeant Kris Knight, course chief of the Yuma predeployment course. I was impressed at the relative speed of the public affairs department. But this call had nothing to do with the PA. Gunny had seen the e-mails going through about my request, and he said he realized it would be "a long time, if ever" before I would get to visit the course. He checked in with Captain Bowe, the officer in charge of the school, to see if the rules could be bent a little to get me in. Bowe's offices are at Fort Leonard Wood in Missouri. "It's hard to be in charge of it from sixteen hundred miles away, that's why I need Gunny Knight," he would later tell me.

"With Gunny Knight in charge, I have the most winning guy I can have in the marines for this job. To use a sports analogy, he's my Tom Brady, Alex Rodriguez, and Michael Jordan all rolled into one. He's what makes this course the winning game it is," Bowe said.

He acknowledged that Knight doesn't always follow every rule. "Sometimes there are black areas in life, sometimes white, sometimes gray. If Gunny ever needs to get into the gray area, he'll dip in and get out as fast as possible. It's always for a good reason."

So Gunny dipped into the gray, and Bowe looked at my request and told Gunny to go ahead. I visited two separate times over the summer. During my August visit, a public affairs guy from YPG drove up to us, and Gunny quietly told me to take a little walk, that he would take care of things. The PA was not happy I was there, Gunny reported, but he didn't have me escorted off the property.

Official approval remains in the works.

★ ★ ★ **26** ★ ★ ★

GUNNY

K ristopher Knight grew up in a small suburban unincorpo-rated community called Camp Dennison, near Cincinnati, Ohio. The camp for which the place is named had been a major army center during the Civil War. Lincoln is purported to have stayed in the house around the corner from Knight's house.

When he was eleven months old, Gunny's black mother and white father divorced. She took the kids and moved in with her parents. Gunny describes his dad as a "redneck guy, and an alco-holic. He could only teach me three things: hunting, shooting, and fishing." There was a falling-out seven years ago, and he hasn't spo-ken to his father since.

His grandfather, who held down two jobs, became a father fig-ure to him very early on. "I grew up on the black side of the family and have my grandfather's hardworking values at my core," he says. "He was my role model." When his mother was able to move out on her own, the young Knight—age six—refused to go with her. His grandfather told her, "It's not negotiable. He stays." That was that.

His mother remarried when Knight was eleven, and she told him that he had to go with the new family to live in New Jersey. He said he wanted to stay with his grandparents. His grandfather once again went to bat for him, and Knight stayed put.

At age fourteen, Knight learned how to drive and would take care of car maintenance and drive the little family Honda Civic around the area with his grandfather's blessing. His grandparents had two rules: Be careful and behave. These came in handy, because Knight loved guns, and his grandfather liked to see a well-behaved boy rewarded with meaningful presents.

There were the usual BB guns, a Crosman pellet gun, a derringer .25 handgun, a Ted Williams .20-gauge shotgun, a Marlin .22 magnum rifle, a Winchester break-barrel .20-gauge shotgun, and a few others. His favorite, though, was a Remington Model 700 .22-250 rifle. He chose it for his eleventh birthday because it had a very large scope. "I had no idea what it was used for until after my grandfather purchased it for me. When I called my father to tell him about it, he informed me that it was the second fastest varmint rifle in the world. I used it for several years to hunt groundhogs. Initially the gun was way too heavy for me, so I used fence posts and the corners of barns to stabilize my shots."

He used his small arsenal for hunting or target shooting. Camp Dennison was surrounded by woods and farm fields, so there was plenty of space for shooting and camping.

If you saw this scene from the outside, you might have been worried, looking into the tent of this well-armed youth. But Knight knew his limits. He kept his firearms in check, didn't get in trouble, and worked hard at side jobs. In a summer job he held at a factory when he was eighteen, he discovered a way to increase the productivity of making valves. It involved cutting down on lag time and using his strength, and not a crane, to hold seventy-five-pound parts. He thought he'd be lauded for it, but other workers were not happy. "Hey, youngblood, you gotta slow down. You're making us look bad," they told him. "No, *you* gotta speed up," he replied.

Even the boss wanted him to put on the brakes and use the approved methods. If nothing else, it was safer. But Knight said he wanted to do it his way because it was the most efficient method and better for the valves themselves, since they didn't run the risk of getting scraped up by the cranes. In the end, the boss had him sign a waiver, and he proceeded.

It would become a common theme in the story of his life, this business of wanting to do what's best and bucking the system if he had to. He went to college for awhile to become a forest ranger, dropped out the day his grandmother died in 1992, and became what he calls a wild child. He rode motorcycles like he was invincible, partied hard, and lived free. In October 1994, a lifelong friend told him he was thinking about joining the marines. They were at a party and very drunk. "He wouldn't stop talking about it, so I said, 'If you'll shut up, and you're serious about joining, I'll join with you.' He was serious and I kept my word." His friend got out after four years, and Gunny's been in since. Knight went the MP route right away. Eight months later, he was at Lackland, learning how to become a handler. Dogs have been his passion ever since.

In the years that followed his enlistment, he rose through the ranks, got a BS in education (he says he could be a captain now, but he would not be able to work with dogs, so he remained a noncommissioned officer; while most of his job these days involves paperwork to keep the program running, he tries to get out with classes whenever possible), had two combat deployments, became a trainer, and in March 2010, came to Yuma to be course chief.

While training with the Israeli Defense Forces in 2006 ("the air force would count that as a combat deployment; I count it as a vacation") he met his future wife, Rinat. I met them for sushi one night in Yuma's nicest shopping center. Rinat Knight is a pretty, funny, smart woman with long, dark, wavy hair, eleven years his junior. He had told me on several occasions, including our first phone conversation, "I am the luckiest man on earth, and a lot of that is because of my wife." She is on one of his two screen savers at work.

Those closest to Gunny in the dog world say he could be in the private sector earning a lot more money than he does in the military. He says he's not going to stay in forever, and in fact, he might retire within a few years. But he has no desire to leave just yet. "I just love what I do. Every day is a Friday. Why would I risk trading my Fridays for a Monday for more money? It's not worth it to me. That's why I do it, and that's why my staff does it.

"I want to make a difference before I leave. I want to make sure all these kids are getting the allotted time to properly prepare and come back home."

Gunny's other screen saver is a photo of him with military working dog Patrick L722. Gunny is running and holding out his arm, which is covered with a bite sleeve, and Patrick is up in the air, biting at it and looking like although he means business, he's having the best time in the world. They are collided, suspended in time in this dynamic photo that greets Gunny every day.

He helped train the handler who would help train Patrick. The dog was fresh out of dog school in Texas when he arrived at Camp Lejeune, North Carolina, to serve with the II Marine Expeditionary Force (II MEF). "He was a hyper mess when we received him, but he showed all the potential to be great," Gunny says. Patrick's handler and Gunny deployed to Afghanistan at the same time in May 2009. While there, Gunny continued to advance the team's capabilities, including trying to make sure Patrick could work off leash.

Patrick made it home and, because his handler needed multiple wrist surgeries, was assigned a new handler. They deployed to Afghanistan in December 2010.

Patrick would not make it back alive this time. But everyone else on his final mission would, thanks to this dog and his ability to sniff out bombs without a leash.

A VERBAL LEASH

Patrick was a bomb-detection dog designed to work on a six-foot leash. Gunny Knight, then chief dog trainer at II MEF, worked hard on Patrick's off-leash skills. Patrick was one of the first PEDD dogs he trained this way. "The barrier had to be broken."

The dog was a typical Malinois. "He was all heart; he put everything into what he did, and he loved you to death," says one marine corporal, who had hoped to deploy with Patrick.

Nothing fazed this dog. During one firefight, Patrick lay beside his handler, Corporal Charles "Cody" Haliscak, in the tall grass as Haliscak and the rest of the squad engaged the Taliban. But Patrick wasn't lying there cowering. He was lying there eating grass as the bullets screamed by.

On May 9, 2011, Patrick and Haliscak were on a mission in the southern Helmand Province. With them were a minesweeper engineer and an explosive ordnance disposal (EOD) technician. The purpose was to check out a small IED—a toe-popper—that had gone off earlier that day. It didn't harm anyone, but they needed a dog's nose to clear the way back to the area. The dog went first, off leash, then the engineer with his metal-detecting device, followed closely by Haliscak and the EOD tech.

It's common knowledge among people who have dealt with IEDs in the last few years that where there's one, there are two. Where there are two, there are four. Knight says the situation has been dramatically worse in recent months. Before, you might find a small field with one IED. Now there could be ten in that same area. (The Yuma course has adjusted training methods to take this lethal factor into account.)

Haliscak had a feeling that something else was out there along their path, and he stopped his team. He told the two men he would let Patrick work this one. Patrick, tail high and wagging, walked up the path, searched one corner of the poppy field that lay ahead, crossed the path, and searched the other end of the poppy field. He shimmied around and made his way to where two paths met— exactly where the team was going to be walking. There, about fifteen feet away from the men, he responded to an explosive scent as Haliscak had never seen him respond before. Patrick's usual style was to get excited, tail wagging hard, sniffing the area with great focus. Then he would sit or lie down in final response. This time, Patrick dispensed with the preliminaries and lay down immediately.

Haliscak figures his dog's last thought was "Oh, toy!!!" ("That toy was everything to him," he says.)

The explosion knocked Haliscak and the two other men off their feet. They had no idea what had happened. They thought they were going to get ambushed, so they prepared to fire. When there was no ambush, Haliscak looked for Patrick. He was nowhere to be seen. The handler started searching in a circle around where the blast had gone off. As a hunter, he is used to looking for downed animals. He peered through his rifle's 4X scope. In the distance he saw that the grass in a field was bent over. Then he saw Patrick's body, or what remained of it.

"At that point I lost it." Haliscak, who had a high-grade concussion from the explosion, tried to run over to his dog, but the EOD tech stopped him. It was enough death for one day. The EOD tech and the engineer got close enough to see there was nothing to be done. They did their post-blast work on the IED and the other one from the morning. It was nearly nighttime when the two men put Patrick on a piece of canvas, covered him up, and carried him back to the patrol base. Haliscak had known the dog for three years, been his handler for one and a half years. "I lost my best friend. He was my hero. Without him and his great ability to work off leash, I'd be toast."

Once they'd brought him back, Haliscak looked at his dog. All four of Patrick's legs had been blown off. Only his head and rib cage were intact. "It's truly terrible to see your best friend like this."

Dual-purpose dogs are officially considered on-leash dogs. It's thought that the patrol part of them is too dangerous to let go off leash, so they don't receive off-leash detection training during boot camp, and often are not even at their home bases. Some handlers work on it on their own—particularly handlers with kennel masters who are wise to its benefits. But it's still far from standard procedure.

Gunny Knight has been working these dual-purpose dogs off

leash for a few years—since before it was even a remotely accepted technique. "I knew this was right. When I know I'm right, a thousand people can think I'm wrong, but I stand alone and know I'm right.

"I believe in a verbal leash. Your leash may be six feet and leather, but mine comes out of my mouth."

Single-purpose bomb dogs, like EDDs, IDDs, TEDDs, and SSDs (see chapter 10 if you have not retained every letter of every acronym of every MWD job) are trained to work off leash. But these are usually sporting breeds, like Labrador retrievers, and they are not trained to attack. They can be trusted not to maul anyone in their path as they trot around sniffing out IEDs.

It's estimated that with our current situation in Afghanistan, about 95 percent of a dual-purpose bomb dog's job is sniffing out explosives—not going after bad guys. Having a bomb-sniffing dog with off-leash capabilities makes sense. The farther from the handler and other troops a dog is when alerting to an IED, the safer for everyone. Except the dog, of course. It's called stand-off distance. Some might argue that this isn't very kind or humane, that these dogs don't realize the dangers and we're sending them out as canaries in a coal mine—almost as sacrifices.

But with the dog out front, even on leash, he's always the most endangered. The idea behind using soldier dogs is that they save lives by detecting explosives before someone can get killed by one. If a dog ends up dying while the men and women behind him live, he will be greatly mourned and remembered as a hero.

Nobody wants to see a dog die. "It just sucks. It's a shitty situation," says Master Chief Thompson. "It hurts a lot. Just about as much as it does to lose a handler."

★

Gunny watches as Navy Master-at-Arms Second Class Joshua Raymond tries working his dog Rex P233 off leash for the first time while looking for roadside explosives. The dog doesn't want to get more than ten feet away from Raymond. The handler explains that he's not allowed to have his dog off leash at his home base.

"We can get another Rex," Gunny tells him, "but we can't get another you. Parents who lose their son or daughter out there, it stays with them for the rest of their life. Children who lose a parent, it's tragic. But tough as it sounds, if your dog dies, sad as that is, you get to come back and take out Flea Biscuit Two and start all over again."

Raymond and Rex walk down the hot dirt road, no shade in sight, just rocks and sand and dried dirt, with the occasional bit of plucky scrub poking through. Rex goes on in front about twelve feet, but then turns around and waits for his handler. The dog is accustomed to feeling the end of the leash well before now.

"Put your toy away, show your dog your hands," shouts out Gunny as Raymond keeps walking. "Tell him 'I don't have it, but there's a way of earning it,' and you gotta send him back down there. Good boy, keep going, good boy, keep going! Don't let him think for himself! Find that command, maybe it's 'forward,' maybe it's 'go,' use your body and step into him. The dog doesn't know he's allowed to be that far away. There you go!

"Now back up! Now the dog takes a picture and, hey! I can be away! He can go twenty-five feet and you can back up twenty-five feet, and now you have fifty feet between you."

About twenty minutes into it, the dog looks like he's getting kind of used to the idea of being off leash. He's walking down the road and off to the sides with more confidence, not stopping so often to wait for his handler. "They all want to be free, with a little guidance, of course," says Gunny. "No one wants to have something tugging on their neck all the time."

Raymond is clearly impressed with what his dog has been able to do. But it goes so much against the navy protocol he has been trained to follow that he can't imagine being able to "get away with" using it.

Gunny explains that inside the wire (on an FOB), leashes are mandatory. "But I'm here to tell you for a fact that you are authorized to not only work your dog off leash here, but also when you go outside the wire in Afghanistan. If anything ever happens, call Master Chief Thompson. I guarantee he'll offer his career to back you up. So will I.

"If you find something out there, no one's going to be like 'Hey, leash up!' I guarantee, in fact, that you will get an extra scoop of mashed potatoes and a tent with AC for you and Rex."

Because of the off-leash capabilities being taught here, Gunny and his staff go a step further than the usual deferred response training. When a dog responds to an IED, the people who teach this course don't just want the dog to stay there staring at it until he gets paid. "In the real world, the handler's not going to walk way over to where the dog is responding," Porras says. "The dog has to be able to leave the odor and come back to you. It's safer all the way around."

It's not that hard to teach, as it turns out. The dog gets his million-dollar reward only when he comes back to the handler—and not when he responds to the explosive. Getting strong on the recall command ("Come!") can serve these dogs well for other reasons as well in Afghanistan. Feral and stray dogs are commonplace, and dogs have gone MIA chasing after them. As well, dirt roads can appear seemingly out of nowhere, with surprising traffic.

"You don't want to let your dog be done in by these dangers," Gunny Knight says. "There are enough of those as it is. A whole lotta shit can go wrong out there."

★ ★ ★ 28 ★ ★ ★

HEAT

Air Force Technical Sergeant Adam Miller walks with his German shepherd, Tina M111, down a dirt road toward a small village, rifle poised. On the right, a white mosque topped with blue and gold. A billboard asking for help for Afghan school-children. To the left, a service station with one nonworking gas pump. A crashed, abandoned pickup truck. Up ahead, several mud-walled buildings, some small, a few two-story. A heap of concrete walls from what looks like a bombed-out building. Several stalls making up a tiny marketplace. In the background, intermittent gunfire.

Miller and his dog walk on—Miller wearing full kit, Tina in harness and leash, which attaches somewhere on Miller's beltline so his hands can be free to use his rifle. It's 11 A.M., 114 degrees. Suddenly more gunfire. "The dog's down!" shouts someone on his team, and without hesitating, Miller reaches down to Tina, hoists her over his left shoulder, and with rifle still ready to take out any-one intent on harming him or his dog, moves a little faster now, toward shelter, anything that will protect them while he tries to save her.

Within two minutes, they make it to a cube-shaped mud-and-concrete building—more of a hut, really. They disappear inside.

This was not in the script. What just happened? I jog over to look in through a window opening, and there's Miller crouched over his dog, working furiously to fix her. This was supposed to be a simulation. We're at the Canine Village just a couple hundred meters away from the dog kennels where we started the day at YPG. But there on the ground, incongruously—sickeningly—is Tina's severed leg. It seems to have been blown completely off her body, and there's an IV flowing into it. How in God's name did this happen?

And why would you put an IV in a severed leg, anyway? I try to look at Tina. She is lying down, and the earth beneath her is wet. Miller is wrapping bandages around her and talking to her. I can only see her front end, but her face does not look like the face of a dog whose leg is two feet away from her. Miller moves, and I see that all four limbs are firmly attached to Tina. Then in the corner of the room, I see someone looking on. She offers Miller advice about the wrap. In a moment, she suggests he do something with the IV on what's called a Jerry leg around here.

(A Jerry leg is a realistic, large, furry, fake dog leg that handlers can use for practicing placing IVs, bandaging, splinting, and giving injections. Complete Jerry dogs are also used for training. They have an artificial pulse and expandable lungs for mouth-to-snout resuscitation. There are also dogs that can be intubated, but the program doesn't currently have any of those.)

Predeployment training does not get much more realistic than this. Miller would later tell me that he was exhausted when he got Tina to the building, and his adrenaline was pumping almost as it would have in a real-life war emergency with Tina. "It's the best canine training I've ever had. The hardest, too," he says. "If this doesn't prepare you for Afghanistan, nothing will."

The woman who is helping Miller patch up his dog is Army Captain Emily Pieracci. She is a veterinarian, and one of her main jobs is to prepare handlers here in every aspect of emergency care possible, as well as in the prevention of problems to begin with. She also makes sure all dogs who come through here are ready for deployment—medically fit and not suffering from heat casualties.

Pieracci grew up with dogs. Her mother was a police dog handler for the Washington State Patrol. Pieracci graduated Washington State University's veterinary school in 2009 and spent several months working in the private sector in the field of emergency medicine in order to pay back her student loans.

She joined the army in 2010. She has found her calling. "The army offered something different from regular civilian practice. I got to jump out of airplanes, shoot weapons, and get lost doing land navigation. I could be a vet and also do a lot of active stuff that didn't involve veterinary medicine." (The army also repaid her vet school loans, which in this economy was a huge blessing.)

Within her first month at Yuma, she knew this was the place for her. She loves working with the handlers and their dogs. "I could not imagine being anywhere else other than the military. To me, this job carries so much meaning. I have such a strong sense of purpose when I care for these dogs. Keeping them healthy saves our troops' lives. It's both powerful and humbling all at the same time."

Pieracci enjoys the heat here, too. But it's this very heat that can also do in the best dogs. Heat injuries among working dogs are not uncommon here or at Lackland or in Afghanistan. On warm days, handlers take their dogs' temperatures (rectally, with digital thermometers; a dog's normal body temperature is between about 101 and 102.5) every two hours, sometimes more. But temperature tolerance can vary greatly. It's not necessarily how hot the dogs get, but how well they can compensate. One MWD went down out here at only 104. Some dogs hit 109 and do fine after they get cooled off quickly. It all depends on the individual dog. Just as important an indicator as temperature, or more so, is how a dog acts.

As Pieracci explains it, heat injury has three categories: heat stress, heat exhaustion, and heat stroke. The signs progress very rapidly, and heat stress and heat exhaustion can be missed by handlers if they are not looking for these. Heat stroke is the most severe form. Signs include rectal temps above 108, unwillingness to work, lethargy, vomiting, diarrhea, uncontrolled panting, and seizures.

Reaching a level defined as heat stroke is different for every dog. But most military working dogs have very high drive, which works against those looking out for them; these dogs would rather work than not. That means handlers have to be extremely vigilant for early warning signs.

Dogs here always have patches shaved on their front legs. That's for easier access to the cephalic vein if a dog goes down during training. It's a precautionary measure Pieracci takes to save time in the field during an emergency, and she encourages handlers to shave this area every two weeks while deployed. She uses the vein to administer IV fluids, which help cool the dog quickly, support stable blood pressure, and help avoid shock. On deployment, if no medics or vets are around, the handler will have to do this. That's why they insert all IVs during veterinary procedures. It helps keep them ready just in case they need to act quickly on their own.

Pieracci says that dogs who go through Yuma tend to fare better with heat injuries downrange than other MWDs. That's mostly due to handler knowledge. Part of the reason the dogs train out here is to show handlers what their dogs look like when they're getting hot: Does the dog seek shade? Does she quit working, or will she keep working no matter how hot it gets? Having the handlers see how their dogs react in Yuma helps them identify when their dog might be overheating in Afghanistan.

Coming to Yuma also makes handlers hyperaware of the need to check dog trailers every ten minutes to ensure the air-conditioning is working when dogs are inside. (It's not very cold air, but just enough to make it somewhat comfortable—or at least tolerable.) "There's a side of me no one wants to see if you kill your dog in one of these," Gunny says as he knocks on an empty trailer.

In late September 2011, two marine IDDs were being transported to Yuma from Fort Bragg, North Carolina. The contractors (the dogs were not with their handlers) responsible for the dogs' care during transport stopped overnight in Phoenix and allegedly left the dogs in the travel trailer unattended. They found IDD Ace dead the next morning, and IDD Max was in critical condition.

According to Pieracci, Max was taken to a Phoenix emergency veterinary hospital, where he received three blood transfusions and massive amounts of fluid and medication. He was in kidney failure and bleeding internally from the heat stroke. He was severely dehydrated, and the vets were worried about his brain swelling from the high levels of sodium in his blood. He remained in critical condition for ten days, but he pulled through.

"He was a real fighter. He was discharged just three days ago and is on his way to Lackland, where he will most likely be adopted out. I don't think he'll ever be able to deploy to a hot environment again after the severity of his case. He may have some long-term kidney and brain damage, and quite frankly, he's been through enough," says Pieracci. "He deployed in 2009 and 2010, and I know he served his country honorably. He deserves a nice comfy couch for as long as he's got left, if you ask me." She has never met Max, but she was on the phone with the Phoenix vets every two to four hours while he fought back from the brink of death. "I feel quite attached to him even though I've never met him. I would love to meet him before he retires, but I'm not sure that will happen."

Those contractors may want to stay out of Gunny Knight's way.

29

THE END OF THE ROAD?

More parachutists drop in front of us as we round a bend later toward the kennels. "Hollywood, that's what they are," Gunny spits.

"I don't know how many frickin' millions of dollars they spend every year to let these guys jump out of planes. Dogs save so many lives out there, this course has saved untold numbers, and as of now, we have no funding after October 2012."

Finally, perhaps, we've come to the reason he feels disdain for the jumpers.

It costs the DOD about $750,000 a year to run the IASK Course. Some 225 handlers go through the course annually. Despite the tremendous (if unquantifiable) success of the course, it's on the chopping block because of the same major budget cuts causing pain everywhere in the military. The program is currently considered a Tier III course, which means it's looked at as "extra" in times of budget crises.

But what is $750,000 when it comes to saving lives? If you have to put a life in terms of dollars, it costs the government $400,000 to

$500,000 in death benefits for every soldier, sailor, airman, or marine killed in action. The Defense Department would have been shelling out more money for the lives Patrick saved that day than it costs to run the IASK Course for an entire year.

"It's astronomical the number of lives that are being saved because of this Yuma program," says Bowe. "And I will panhandle to get this if I have to."

The idea is for the course—which began in late 2005 as an "urgent need" program—to become a formal, required course. This would guarantee funding for awhile. Bowe had exhausted two of three options by the time this book went to press. "The program absolutely must not, cannot go away," Bowe says. "Too many people and dogs will die."

I would not be surprised if dogs around here smell a little extra fear these days.

30

THE SCIENTISTS WEIGH IN
ON NOSE POWER

The mind of a soldier, the nose of a trained dog: a perfect partnership," dog behaviorist and anthrozoologist John Bradshaw wrote me one day during a round of e-mails about a dog's sense of smell. It was a refreshing change from the mound of complex scientific journal articles that had accumulated on my desk about the subject of a dog's sense of smell, including one I was trying to get through at the moment: "The Fluid Dynamics of Canine Olfaction: Unique Nasal Airflow Patterns as an Explanation of Macrosmia."

If dogs had noses like yours or mine, they would have an utterly different and diminished role in today's military. The Department of Defense would still likely use some dogs for patrol purposes (although there are currently no "patrol only" dogs), but as it is now, those skills are rarely called upon. And say what you will about companionship or the value of a unit having another set of eyes, we are involved in a war where IEDs are the number one killer. If soldier dogs didn't have such excellent noses, they would be a rare breed.

Dog owners are all too aware that there's something different about the way dogs sense the world. For instance, there's the old "Nice to meet you! Now I'll sniff your crotch and learn more about you!" business that embarrasses many of us when we have company over. And it's a dog's sense of smell that's at least partly responsible for why walks that would take ten minutes without a dog take at least twice as long (especially with a male dog) if you let the dog set the tempo. On walks, I find myself asking Jake things like "How could you possibly smell that tuft of grass for an entire minute? Can't you see it's just grass?"

In a way, dogs are wonderful travel companions because they do force you to slow down from the madcap pace many of us maintain on vacation. We try to fit in too many activities, too many sites, and then we return feeling more exhausted than when we left.

With a dog, though, you have to stop the car more frequently than you might normally, so the dog can have a bathroom break and stay comfortable. And you can't just race around from one attraction to another when you're hoofing it with a dog. A dog will, by his very nature, force you to slow down a bit. In other words, to use a cliché I have used too many times in my talks: Dogs help you stop and smell the roses.

I never really thought too much about the literal meaning of a dog smelling a rose until I came across this description by Alexandra Horowitz in her wonderful book *Inside of a Dog: What Dogs, See, Smell, and Know*:

Imagine if each detail of our visual world were matched by a corresponding smell. Each petal on a rose may be distinct, having been visited by insects leaving pollen footprints from faraway flowers. What is to us just a single stem actually holds a record of who held it, and when. A burst of chemicals marks where a leaf was torn. The flesh of the petals, plump with mois- ture compared to that of the leaf, holds a different odor besides. The fold of a leaf has a smell; so does a dew drop on a thorn. And time is in those details: while we can see one of the petals drying and browning, the dog can smell this process of decay and aging.

Since reading that passage, and learning a great deal about dogs' sense of smell, I have been more understanding when Jake stops and spends a full minute inspecting a neighbor's hedge. I am so awed by what a dog's nose is capable of, in fact, that I try to add a little time to our walks so I don't have to rush him from his rich world of fascinating odors. That hedge is imbued with odors rep- resenting many things, including all the dogs who have preceded Jake. "Dogs read about the world through their noses, and they write their messages, at least to other dogs, in their urine," psychol- ogist and prolific dog-book author Stanley Coren told me. Who am I to tear Jake away from his favorite news and gossip blog?

I'm now also slightly less discomfited when Jake and another dog greet each other by heading right for each other's nether regions. Chances are the dogs are learning far more about each other than the other dog's owner and I are learning about each other; we make idle chitchat and try very hard not to notice our dogs' utter fascina- tion with each other's anal area and sexual organs; exactly what the dogs are learning about each other, and what they do with that information, has yet to be figured out by science. But it's very likely far beyond "Nice weather we're having, eh?" "Yup, how 'bout them

Giants?" It's probably more along the lines of "How old are you, and what's your personality like, and what did you have for dinner, and are you gonna be nice or a jerk?"

The canine proclivity for sniffing out what we might consider the more intimate olfactory signals may have helped the Allies in World War II: Nazis stationed along the Maginot Line were using dogs as messengers. French soldiers attempted to shoot the dogs, but the dogs were quick and stealthy.

Enter a French femme fatale. She was a little thing, a messenger dog who had just gone into heat. She went on her mission, and when she returned to her post that evening, about a dozen German military dogs were close behind. It was a small victory played out in the battlefields. *Toujours l'amour.*

Figures abound about how much better a dog's sense of smell is than ours. There are so many variables that it's almost impossible to quantify. I've seen figures indicating that it's from 10 to 100 to 1,000 to 1,000,000 times better. Bradshaw explains that dogs can detect some, if not most, odors at concentrations of parts per trillion. The human nose, by contrast, is lucky to get into the parts-per-billion range and is often relegated to parts per million. That makes a dog's nose between 10,000 to 100,000 times more sensitive than ours. The range is obviously very wide, and the sensitivity depends on variables like the dog and the odor. Research continues.

Coren gives an example of what this extra sensitivity looks like. Let's say you have a gram of a component of human sweat known as butyric acid. Humans are quite adept at smelling this, and if you let it evaporate in the space of a ten-story building, many of us would still be able to detect a faint scent upon entering the building. Not bad, for a human nose. But consider this: If you put the 135-square-mile city of Philadelphia under a three-hundred-foot-high enclosure, evaporated the gram of butyric acid, and let a dog in, the average dog would still be able to detect the odor.

If a dog can detect BO in such tiny amounts, imagine what it's like for a dog to be immersed in a world of sweaty humans in a far smaller space. Coren was recently able to observe one of his dogs in just such a situation, when he was out picking up a friend at the gym. He brought along Ripley, his young Cavalier King Charles spaniel, whom he held in his arms. When they entered the gym, Ripley's nose flew up in the air and he went stiff—a clear-cut case of olfactory overload.

This same dog would go on to nearly blind Coren in one eye the week before we spoke in October 2011. Coren had fallen asleep in his favorite chair. The nine-month-old Ripley, being both a lap dog and a face-licker, took advantage of the moment and, in the process of enthusiastically slathering Coren's face, got one of his nails lodged in the inner margin of Coren's left eye. The dog, unable to extract it, used his other paw to press against Coren to dislodge it. When I interviewed him, Coren's eye had ruptured, the iris and the lens were gone. He'd had two surgeries, with two or three more to go "before they give up," he said. He takes it in stride. He would have started to go blind in that eye from a progressive eye disorder within a couple of years anyway, so he says the dog just speeded up the process. I wondered if maybe the dog had some sense of his eye problem and was trying to help him, like dogs I have read about who try to chew away cancerous moles. Coren, perhaps not surprisingly, does not give Ripley any accolades as a diagnostician or surgeon.

A handy way a dog's olfactory sensitivity manifests itself is with something called odor layering. This enables a dog to separate a chosen scent from the "background noise" of all the other scents, much as humans could visually sort a bunch of miscellaneous items spread out on the ground. Dog handlers have variations of analogies for odor layering, and they're all based on food. Probably the most common: We humans can smell the pizza. A dog can smell the dough, the sauce, the cheese, and all the spices and toppings. A dog might even be able to smell the components of each of those. Not just dough, but flour and yeast. Not just sauce, but tomatoes and basil and oregano. Some handlers and dog trainers use chocolate cake as an example, others use stew. But it all boils down to the fact that dogs have very sensitive noses that are capable of teasing apart scents as you and I could never dream of doing.

As Navy Lieutenant Commander John Gay was driving me to the submarine in Norfolk to see little Lars do his detection work, he told me that even his late boxer, Boris, was adept at odor layering in his heyday. (Boxers are generally not renowned sniffers.) Gay's wife used to bake all kinds of muffins and cookies, and Boris would show no interest. But when she made a particular kind of cookie that Boris was allowed to eat, he waited eagerly by the oven door, even though she gave no indication the cookies were for him. Oh, and the dog could also smell flies. Flies.

We humans have, not surprisingly, found plenty of ways to put this exquisitely sensitive olfactory apparatus to work in detecting odors of importance to us. Some of them seem nothing but miraculous.

Dogs are proving very adept at sniffing out a variety of cancers, including lung, ovarian, skin, and colon malignancies. Specially trained dogs can predict seizures in those prone to them, or sense dangerous changes in blood sugar levels in diabetics. Dogs can detect pests, including bedbugs and termites. They've been used to sniff out cell phones in prisons, oil and gas pipeline leaks, flammable liquid traces in arson investigations, toxic molds, diseases in beehives, and contraband foodstuffs. They can tell when a cow is going into heat. They can even use their noses to find cash. Jake has shown no talent for this I'm afraid.

Former Marine Sergeant Brandon Liebert, whom you may remember from an earlier chapter (his dog, Monty, found six hundred rounds of antiaircraft ammunition), was stationed at Cherry Point, North Carolina, in 2005. One day he sent out a dog team to sweep the convention center in Morehead City prior to a Marine Corps Ball. The team went out on what was a formality. But a few hours later Liebert received a call to say that the dog had responded to something in one part of the convention site. Verification was required. Liebert was the only handler available, so he got Monty and rushed off to investigate.

"When we got to the area of where the other dog had responded, Monty began to circle the room multiple times and then finally stopped in the middle of the room. I asked the handler what his dog did, and the handler stated that his dog had responded on the tables behind me. We got out of the area and informed the local authorities."

It would later turn out that there had been a Ducks Unlimited show the previous weekend and that there were a lot of guns and ammunition for sale. The vendors had placed the ammunition on tables, and so it was a residual odor the dogs had picked up on. The ball went on as planned.

★ ★ ★ 31 ★ ★ ★

A TOUR OF A DOG'S NOSE

Not all dogs have the same genius for sniffing. Dogs with longer snouts generally have more sensitive noses than dogs with stubby noses, like bulldogs. This is one of the reasons why you will probably never see a pug as a military working dog, unless the military decides it needs something rather amusing-looking to distract the enemy.

Let's see why size matters. If you have more odor analyzers in your nose, you are going to be more sensitive to smell. We humans have about five million odor receptors in our noses. The area these take up if unfurled would be about the size of a postage stamp. Dogs with long noses have far more of these scent receptors. Dachshunds have 125 million. But German shepherds have 225 million of them. So do beagles, which is pretty amazing considering they're half the size of shepherds. Bloodhounds have the most, with three hundred million. A bloodhound's olfactory receptor area is about the size of a handkerchief. (You will not see bloodhounds in the military, though. Doc Hilliard explains that while they have great noses, and can be excellent trackers, most do not retrieve or play with Kongs or balls the way they need to for the training. I wonder if another reason could be that their droopy, drooly countenances don't seem very "military.")

Smell is the dominant sense in dogs—even in those with less prominent snouts. From the outer nose (known as a dog's "leather") to the brain, a dog's olfactory system makes ours look like it needs to go back to the manufacturer. (But our eyes have all the grandeur of their noses, so it all works out.)

Here's a quick look at what happens when a military working dog we'll call Sam, a German shepherd, sniffs an odor of interest; let's say ammonium nitrate. Sam is close to a scent, but not sure quite where it is yet. He sniffs more rapidly, so the air coming into his nose is more turbulent and more of it can be distributed onto his olfactory membranes. He can sniff up to twenty times for every exhalation if he's really interested in a scent. He can even pull a neat trick of inhaling at the same time he exhales. And he can move his nostrils independently, which helps him figure out just where a scent is coming from. When Sam thinks that he may be quite near the source, he will sniff more deeply, actively drawing air over the source to confirm its location. At this point he may even be able to compare the concentration of odor between left and right nostrils, which will both confirm that the source is nearby and further help to pinpoint its location.

As he sniffs, scent molecules stick to the moisture on Sam's nose. (The moisture is actually mucus, which helps snortle the molecules all the way through the olfaction process.) Scent molecules dissolve in the mucus, and the sniffing carries them into the nose, to two bony plates called turbinates. This is the home of those millions of scent-detecting cells discussed earlier.

Adding to Sam's nasal prowess is a body part that doesn't seem to exist in any functional form in humans: an extra olfactory chamber known as the vomeronasal organ, aka Jacobson's organ. It's located above the roof of a dog's mouth, just behind the upper incisors. It has ducts that open to the nose and mouth so scent molecules can be processed. Most mammals and reptiles have a vomeronasal organ. It's used primarily to detect pheromones (not terribly helpful for Sam on the job), but some scientists think it may have other functions we're not yet aware of.

The brains of dogs and people and most vertebrates contain two structures called olfactory bulbs, which help us decode smells. The olfactory bulbs of dogs are about four times as big as those of people, despite the fact that dogs' brains are far smaller than ours. Between this and his 225 million scent receptors, Sam is able to find the ammonium nitrate quickly. He sits, stares, and is called back by his handler, who gives him his cherished Kong and praises him up like mad.

All in a day's work for a good nose.

Oh, and lest you think it's all about sniffing and letting nature take it from there, a dog also has to do a great deal of legwork to locate an odor. Bradshaw explains that a dog's first strategy is to run cross-wind to figure out whether or not he is directly downwind of the source. But wind spreads scent in unpredictable ways, so this may not be very informative. If the scent is continuous, the source must be very close by, so the wind direction is an unreliable clue, and visual cues may provide the best indication of the source. If the scent is discontinuous, its source is probably some distance away, so the dog will briefly switch to proceeding upwind; if the scent is quickly lost, he will switch back to running cross-wind to try to position himself more precisely in the odor "corridor." Then, switching between upwind and cross-wind running will bring the dog, somewhat crabwise, to within close range of the source.

But what if the scent itself is moving?

A CLOUD OF SCURF

In the silence of the vast desert, you can hear the *chop-chop* of the marine UH-1 helicopter (aka a Huey) approaching for miles. It comes near and veers suddenly, looping in quick semi-amusement-park fashion, circles overhead again, and descends. As it nears the ground, a fast-moving cloud of dust and tiny pebbles races toward Gunny Knight and me, dinging my camera lens and making it impossible to keep our eyes open for the next several seconds.

The air remains thick with dust when out of the helicopter, whose rotors are still churning, run a dog and handler, followed by another dog team. The handlers hunch forward slightly as they run, to better protect themselves from the churning sand and air. They race off into the distance, then stop. The dogs sniff the ground with great interest, but just then the helicopter lifts off, and we lose sight of everything again.

Gunny and I catch up with these teams, and a few others, while they're resting up after having tracked a "bad guy" varying distances at the Yuma Proving Ground. The dogs are combat tracker dogs. While explosives dogs find bombs, these dogs find the people who plant them. (In friendly operations, they can track down lost people.) The dogs here today are training for real-life combat missions, which often involve these rapid helicopter drops. The dogs need to get used to these so they're ready when they deploy.

One of the dogs was so scared of the helicopter this day that he put the brakes on as he approached it and had to be nearly carried aboard. He spent the ride with his head tucked firmly into the crotch of his handler, who had to move her rifle to make room for him. (Once off the helicopter, though, he tracked his man beautifully, I'm told.) Most dogs stayed very close to their handlers, and hunkered down and strapped in, for the ride. One veteran dog took in the view from the helicopter's edge while firmly grasped by his handler.

These dogs are trained to track human odor over distances. They pick up a scent where a handler "suggests" (near an IED, for instance, or the last place an insurgent stood) and follow it. Tracks can be miles long and hours—or even days—old. Recall James Earl Ray, who broke out of a Tennessee prison in 1977 and was pursued by sister bloodhounds named Sandy and Little Red. They started their manhunt days after his escape, but within a few hours they had found him a mere three miles away. (Now *there* are a couple of hound dogs who could do the job.)

Tracking dogs keep their heads down and follow the scent on the ground. The track is a combination of human scent and crushed vegetation or stirred-up dirt or sand. Disturbed environments, like crushed grass (the grass "bleeds," in a sense), give off unique smells. But nothing as unique as the smell of the person being pursued.

You may think that if you shower well and wear deodorant, you smell like just about everyone else out there. But our individual scent fingerprints are unique. As Horowitz says, "To our dogs, we *are* our scent."

Anyone who is thinking of outwitting a tracking dog one day should read what she has to say about our scents:

> *Humans stink. The human armpit is one of the most profound sources of odor produced by any animal; our breath is a confusing melody of smells; our genitals reek. The organ that covers our body—our skin—is itself covered in sweat and sebaceous glands, which are regularly churning out fluid and oils holding our particular brand of scent. When we touch objects, we leave a bit of ourselves on them; a slough of skin, with its clutch of bacteria steadily munching and excreting away. This is our smell, our signature odor.*

Coren likens our shedding skin cells to the *Peanuts* character Pigpen, who always has a visible billow of dirt around him. It seems humans have the same billow, only it's made up of skin cells, which when in this flake form are known as rafts or scurf. We shed fifty million skin cells each minute. That's a lot of scurf. "They fall like microscopic snowflakes," Coren says. Thankfully, we can't see this winter wonderland ourselves. But these rafts or scurf, with their biological richness, including the bacteria that sheds with them, are very "visible" to dogs' noses.

Where a dog begins on a track is naturally where the scent is weakest, because it's been there longest. As the track progresses in the right direction, the scent should get stronger. The increasing strength of a track is something dogs rely on. "They start at the far-thest point in the past and work their way up, we hope, to the present moment, where they find who they're tracking," says Marine Corporal Wesley Gerwin, course chief/instructor supervisor for the combat tracker course. "It's sort of like a dog's version of time travel."

Dry heat and ultraviolet light can cause a track to disintegrate quickly. Moisture and lack of sun help preserve tracks. Even if someone tries to throw a dog off the scent by going through a stream or river, there's still likely to be a track. In most cases, if the dog is not too far behind, the water will not erase the scent. In fact, breezes can waft a person's scent to a moist riverbank, where it can remain for a long time. (If a river is flowing very quickly and is rel-atively shallow, though, the scent dissipates far more swiftly.)

There aren't many combat tracking dogs in the military. The numbers are in the low dozens, but security concerns preclude a more precise count. CTD handlers have to have been military working dog handlers for a minimum of a year; they then spend six additional weeks in a CTD course—four weeks at Lackland, two weeks at Yuma. The dogs are trained as combat trackers from the start. They begin tracking at distances of a foot or two (a second or two old) and work their way up. The oldest recorded track since the CTD program started in its most recent incarnation a few years ago is seventy-two hours, in Al Anbar Province, Iraq. Gerwin says he's heard talk of a track up to five days old, but it's not official.

$$\bigstar \ \bigstar \ \bigstar \ \mathbf{33} \ \bigstar \ \bigstar \ \bigstar$$

DOG SENSE

In addition to their stellar noses, combat tracking dogs, like all military dogs, rely on other senses to do their jobs. Phenomenal as their noses are, soldier dogs can't go purely by scent. A combat tracker, for instance, will use his eyes and ears to pinpoint his target as he approaches it. Patrol dogs depend a great deal on hearing and eyesight as well, especially when it comes to detecting the subtle movements or sounds of a suspect.

Like their noses, dogs' ears are significantly more sensitive than ours, especially at high frequencies. "Dogs would describe us as having high-frequency deafness," writes Bradshaw in his book *Dog Sense*. In the Pacific Islands during World War II, soldier dogs could sometimes detect the thin wires on booby traps by the very high-pitched whine produced when air moved over them. Some dogs ended up being trained in just this sort of sound detection. (The sound was utterly inaudible to any humans nearby.)

Canine ears have a reputation of being able to hear sounds up to four times farther than ours can. The mobility of their ears plays a role in helping locate and focus on sounds. As anyone who has ever watched a dog listen to something of great interest will tell you, a dog's ears almost seem to have minds of their own. It's no wonder: Dogs have about eighteen muscles helping them swivel and tilt their ears in response to sound. It's pretty endearing to watch. Jake is adept at this ear maneuver whenever he begs for food or sits in the backyard listening for the cat.

Dogs have poor color vision compared to ours, decent night vision, and generally see a wider picture than we do because of the placement of their eyes. But how a dog sees the world is highly dependent on what a dog looks like. Dogs with longer noses, like most military working dogs, tend to have more photoreceptors crowded together in a horizontal streak across the eye. This "visual streak," as it's called, makes for better panoramic vision, with a field of vision that extends up to about 240 degrees (as opposed to our full frontal 180). Dogs with this kind of vision can even have some awareness of what's going on behind them. But don't ask them to focus on anything closer than ten to fifteen inches in front of their noses. Their eyes aren't set up for that kind of vision. Dogs with shorter noses likely do better with closer vision. Their vision cells are packed in more of a circular shape, making for a narrower field of vision and more visual acuity up front.

This may explain why retrievers retrieve and lapdogs, with their big forward-looking eyes and their small snouts, like to sit on your lap and look at you.

Scientists are continuing to investigate the eyes, ears, and noses of dogs. And beyond the realm of these senses, they're reaching out to get to know more about dog psychology, including how dogs think, feel, solve problems, and why they behave the way they do. Canine cognition is a relatively new field that's burgeoning with enthusiastic scientists eager to plumb dogs' minds for things we've wondered about but never explored before.

PLUMBING A DOG'S MIND

The heart of the Duke Canine Cognition Center is the dog lab. Unlike many laboratories that use dogs as guinea pigs for research, there is no pain in this lab. There aren't even cages. In fact, the lab looks like a small dance studio. The white floor is striped with an assortment of tape colors; red, green, yellow, and blue. The dogs who come here enter with their owners, stay within feet of their owners, leave with their owners, and inevitably get treats and lots of attention during the studies. It's Center Director Brian Hare's idea of "an awesome place to learn about dogs."

It's late morning, and Hare, assistant professor of evolutionary anthropology and cognitive neuroscience, warns me that he just had cake from Costco and a coffee. "I'm totally ADD, I warn you. I'm really excited about a lot of things," he tells me, blue eyes glittering. For the next hour, Hare talks fast and nonstop about the dog lab as he careens about his office. There's something about his energy, his look, and demeanor that keeps reminding me of Brendan Fraser's George of the Jungle—only Hare's rendition holds advanced degrees, has earned great respect in the world of academia, and has the tremendous responsibility that goes along with founding and running a major research facility at one of the nation's top universities.

This lab is one of a few dog cognition labs that have opened at universities in the United States in the last several years, including one run by Alexandra Horowitz at Barnard College. Until the late 1990s, little attention was paid to the topic of canine cognition. Primates were the primary animals being studied for cognition. But "now it's like out-of-control exciting, trying to unlock the secrets of a dog's mind. Now everybody is so super-excited by this research on dogs, from psychologists to anthropologists to the average American dog lover," Hare says as he swipes his hands through his shock of thick, wavy hair.

Hare and his staff had just written a grant to the Department of Defense when I visited. He admits he's never worked with military dogs before, but he has many ideas about how his center can help advance the understanding of dogs in a way he thinks would benefit the military dog program. He'd like to develop a cognitive test for dogs who have been involved in stressful situations, like deployments. He also wants to be able to put together a system so handlers can check their dogs for stress in the field by methods other than simply looking at behavior. This involves testing cortisol levels in conjunction with core body temperatures, as taken by a thermal imaging temperature gun.

In addition, he'd eventually like to be able to use the results of an ongoing study on something called "laterality bias" to help improve accuracy of detector dogs. "Dogs tend to go to the right. A lot tend to stay to the right of what they're searching," Hare explains. "It's something you should know about your dog before you send him to find explosives, if he favors one side over the other. Don't you think that's important information?"

I'm not sure what the Department of Defense thinks of Hare's ideas, but even if he doesn't get the grant the first time, the DOD should be prepared for more grant proposals in the future. "We want to help save money and dogs and save lives, and we'll keep trying," Hare says.

He and his graduate students are running several studies concurrently. This helps explain the colorful stripes and circles and geometric figures all over the floor of the lab. In certain studies, dogs and people need to be at certain fixed places. Marking up the floor eliminates a variable. The green tape is for the predictions study, the yellow tape is for the inhibitory control study, the worn-out blue tape is for a completed attention study, and the red tape is for the trust study.

The red tape is where we find Alice and Duane Putnam, who have driven for two hours to get here from Warren County, on the border of Virginia and North Carolina. (Staffers here tell me that they get calls from dog lovers all over the world who want to bring their dogs to the lab to be part of the research. The lab tries to limit participants to no more than a three-hour drive, so the dog won't be discombobulated by travel.) The Putnams are here with their dog, Tri, who looks like he's part Rottweiler, part German shepherd, and a bit of something else. They believe he is the reincarnation of two of their previous dogs, thus the name. (Two plus himself equals three. Tri sounds better than Three.)

The Putnams are fascinated with their dog. They say he's too smart for his own good. When no one is looking, he opens peanut butter jars and Vaseline jars by screwing off their lids. Then he eats the contents.

Today Tri the Vaseline thief is taking part in the study about trust. He has been here before because his "dog parents," as they call them at the cognition center, like the idea that they're contributing to the better understanding of dogs. Besides, it gets them off their ten acres in the rural corner of the state.

Researcher Jingzhi Tan, aka "Hippo," has devised a study that investigates how trust is established and whether dogs differentiate between owners, a very friendly new acquaintance, and a complete stranger. His goal is actually to find out how humans become friendly and trusting, and he says a good way to study this is through dogs. Many of the studies at the center could end up with significant findings about people as well as dogs.

When I start observing (via a video monitor, so I don't interfere with the goings-on), Tri is being lovingly petted by a new acquaintance—someone who works at the center. She is on the floor with him, making friends like this for about twenty minutes. The Putnams are thrilled Tri is letting a stranger handle him without balking. He's usually not quite as social with people he doesn't know.

Following the petting session, this new friend and a complete stranger will enter the room and take turns sitting next to bowls with food—one bowl will be near the person, one will be near an empty chair. If the dog thinks a person is risky, the idea is that he'd try to avoid that person, and would pick the food that's farther away. Mary, an intern who helps coordinate dog visits here, is the stranger today. But Tri doesn't seem to mind going near her. He is fine with his new friend, too. In other variations of this study, the new friend and stranger take turns pointing to food bowls and researchers see if the dog trusts one more than the other.

The study, and others like it, could eventually have implications for military dogs and how they come to trust their handlers, but that would be years down the road. What counts now in this room is that Tri, dog number 54 for this study, is done and that he has trusted more people than the Putnams would have thought. They proudly stroke his head and tell him, "You did good!"

Alice Putnam exhorts him: "Kissy Mama!" He doesn't. "He's not much of a kisser," she explains. She says she knows her dog well.

But how well does her dog know her? Chances are, much better than she would suspect.

★ ★ ★ 35 ★ ★ ★

THE SMELL OF FEAR REVISITED

Alexandra Horowitz likens dogs to anthropologists: They study us. They observe us. They smell changes in our very chemistry. They learn to predict us. "They know us in ways our human partners sometimes do not," she says.

I've heard a similar refrain dozens of times from handlers, particularly those who have deployed and spent almost every hour for months with their dogs: Their dogs know them better than their spouses or parents do.

Nearly every handler I interviewed, for instance, said that his dog can tell when he's having a bad day. Most civilian dog lovers would say the same thing. But how can it be that a dog—who doesn't speak your language and doesn't know about problems with your bills or your boss or your in-laws—can somehow sense when things are amiss in your life?

It's a phenomenon many military working dog handlers and instructors refer to as "dumping down the leash." How you're feeling and acting is observed by a dog, who will react to this information in different ways. A tense handler is likely to make a dog more tense. Likewise, if a handler is confident and not fearful, even after a loud explosion nearby, the idea is that a dog who is not already gun-shy will figure there's nothing to worry about, with an instinctual logic along the lines of "My handler's OK with it, and he's the leader here, so it must be OK."

Dogs are very sensitive to body language, so the least little tense movement—a change of gait, a slight hunching of shoulders—can be observed and interpreted as something being amiss. When we're upset, our voices can go up slightly in frequency as well. Dogs get these nuances in ways most people don't.

Masking strong feelings by acting like things are OK may not always work, either: It's quite likely that dogs can smell fear, anxiety, even sadness, says Horowitz. The flight-or-fight hormone, adrenaline, is undetectable by our noses, but dogs can apparently smell it. In addition, fear or anxiety is often accompanied by increased heart rate and blood flow, which sends telltale body chemicals more quickly to the skin surface.

It makes for a trifecta of revelations to a dog: a bouquet of visual, auditory, and olfactory cues that makes dogs incredibly tuned in to how we're feeling.

It's comforting to think dogs have empathy and want to see the people they care about feel better when things are not quite right. This sort of action adds to their reputation as man's best friend. But most scientists who study dog behavior say it's more likely that dogs who seem to be acting in comforting, helpful ways simply want to restore order to their pack.

John Bradshaw explained it to me this way: "People are more important to dogs than anything else, and they rely on us to provide them with a stable and predictable social environment. If they sense that anything unusual is going on, that people are behaving in ways they don't usually behave, they will do anything they can to restore the situation.

"Initially they'll do things that have worked in similar situations in the past. They're not trying to comfort anyone else, they're trying to comfort themselves, but often one leads to the other. The dog picks up a toy and uses it to get someone's attention, usually the person who's behaving oddly (as far as the dog is concerned), but not necessarily. The dog is just craving attention—but if it does this in a "cute" way, then the effect may well be to calm that person down. That is in itself rewarding for the dog, so the next time a similar situation presents itself, the dog wheels out the same strategy. It doesn't know why its behavior has the desired effect, it just knows that it works."

It makes sense. And I've heard this from a few different dog experts. But I prefer my own interpretation of Jake's actions when I'm having a rare bad day. He follows me around significantly more, making an extra effort to visit me at my writing desk. He usually leaves me alone here: This is my turf, distraction-free as possible, which is handy on tight deadlines. But on a tough day, Jake will inevitably scratch on my door for admittance. Happy to see a friendly face, I let him in and pet him for awhile. That alone makes me feel better. Then he usually curls up under my desk, falling asleep at my feet.

It may not be scientific, but it feels pretty good to think Jake has empathy. Sometimes he even seems to pick up on my likes and dislikes, favoring the people I enjoy but getting downright testy with one rude man we see sometimes at the park. Whenever we encounter him, this man snarls at me: "Better clean up after your dog, lady." Apparently he does this to all people with dogs. I don't take it personally, but it's annoying.

The first couple of times this happened, I assured him of my poop-scooping vigilance, but now I just try to avoid him when I see him. But sometimes our paths will cross. When they do, Jake does something he doesn't do with 99.9 percent of the people we meet on our walks. He barks. Just a few good deep bellows, followed by a long stare as if to say, "Leave us alone or else." I don't bother telling him to stop. He'll join up with me within moments, and I quietly cheer him on with a "Good boy!" He may not be wearing one, but my feelings have clearly dumped down the leash.

Of course, Gunny Knight could have told you all about dogs' senses long ago without any studies. "I don't need all that scientific stuff. The best lab is right out here with the dogs, and especially over on deployment. That's where dogs and handlers really get to know each other."

PART FOUR

★ ★ ★

DOGS AND
THEIR SOLDIERS

ROUND THE CORNER,

DOWN TO THE RIVER

In February 2011 a marine squad of about twenty men was returning to base in the upper Gereshk Valley of the Helmand Province in Afghanistan after a morning of patrolling a small village. Coalition forces hadn't been in this area for ten years, but they had encountered no problems. They'd walked from the lush "green zone" near the Helmand River up to a plateau in the muddy "brown zone." It was a cold, wet, overcast day and they were glad to be heading back.

Suddenly three Taliban insurgents opened fire with AK-47s from about sixty yards behind them. The marines in the rear immediately whirled around and fired back with M4s, 240s, and 249s, while other marines flanked the insurgents so they wouldn't get away. It's a tactic known as laying a base of fire and enveloping the enemy. It can be highly effective, but this time the insurgents bolted just before the squad could surround them.

The three men ran behind a thick mud wall around a compound at the village edge and once again fired their weapons at the marines, who were in a vulnerable position in a field of short poppies. Several marines ran toward the gunfire, shooting their own weapons in a fast, cyclic manner they'd practiced to perfection. They looked fearless on the outside, but inside, dog handler Marine Sergeant Mark Vierig told himself, "Just don't get shot in the face. Just don't get shot in the face," as they charged the wall, running straight into the fire.

At this point, the insurgents probably realized they did not have fire superiority, and they fled toward the half mile–wide village, hoping to blend in and get lost.

But you don't get lost so easily when there's a combat tracking dog team in hot pursuit. Vierig and his Belgian Malinois, Lex L479, are a rare breed of military dog team. Their mission is twofold: to find the people who plant IEDs and to track down fleeing insurgents who so easily disappear into their familiar surroundings.

Vierig has been a dog handler since 2002 and a combat tracker for the last two years. His dog is six and one of the best noses in the business.

They set out after the men. Any of the three would do. Vierig ran to the spot where he knew one of the men had been, and put his dog on the track, telling him *"Zoeken!"* (Dutch for "Search!"; Lex is from the Netherlands.) Lex picked up the man's scent immediately, and they started following the invisible trail toward the village.

The dog pulled strongly on the leash, nose to the ground, tail up, confident. Vierig followed six to ten feet behind, running in eighty pounds of full combat gear. As long as his dog had his nose down and "pulled like a freight train," Vierig knew he was on track. In situations like this, where people are fleeing from a chase instead of just casually walking away from planting an IED, the track they leave is particularly strongly infused with "extreme pheremones" and other scents that are highly interesting to dogs.

Tracking is a dangerous mission in Afghanistan, where IEDs are so prevalent that troops don't want to go out without a metal detector or a bomb dog. Trackers don't have either luxury. In situations like this, they're heading into virgin territory at a jog or even a run. If a dog loses the track, and a handler doesn't realize it, not only may the two lose their quarry, but they can lose their lives— and those of the troops following close behind.

But if the dog is on a good track, it's a safer business. After all, the person the dog is pursuing has already run over the ground and would (in theory) have set off any IEDs. Plus the insurgents are often very aware of where IEDs are and will avoid those areas. (Much intel on IED placement is gathered by observing insurgents and others steering clear of certain areas.)

Lex continued into the village in confident pursuit of the insurgent. It's tricky tracking around buildings, because there are many places for the enemy to hide and open fire. So once in the village, Vierig had to slow down his dog and begin doing tactical tracking. Slowing the pace increases the time/distance gap that's important to keep to a minimum when tracking, but it's the only way to proceed in villages. For instance, Vierig explains, there's the matter of corners. Danger can literally lurk around every one of them.

"If I blow by a corner and the guy knows I'm tracking him, he can just hide behind a corner and as I blow by straight, he can shoot me. So I'll get to the corner of the building, down the dog, pie the corner [a tactic where a handler can look around the corner in cautious "slices" to make sure no one is waiting to kill] and if it's clear, we move on."

Lex and Vierig tracked the man through the labyrinth of alleys in the village. People who had been out when the marines had patrolled the village earlier had all run inside for safety. The village appeared eerily devoid of residents. Lex didn't lose the scent trail once. The insurgent wasn't in sight, but he may as well have been. Lex's nose could "see" his trail as clearly as you and I can see a path in a park.

Lex suddenly took an abrupt right turn down an alleyway. The dog "threw a huge change of behavior," picking up his head a little higher, pulling to the point where Vierig couldn't stop him. "OK, boys," he yelled to the eight marines who were keeping up right behind him in perfect Ranger file, "we're close, get ready."

At the end of the alley, Vierig could see the man for the first time since he ran behind the wall. He was bent over a creek, rubbing his hands with water, presumably in an effort to remove any scent of black powder. As they approached, Lex barked "in a way that hits a nerve in my neck," says Vierig. The man had nowhere to run. The marines snapped some flex-cuffs on him and radioed the others in the squad to take him. Vierig gave Lex loads of praise, lots of pats and rubs, and threw him a tennis ball, which he joyously destroyed. "His tennis ball is like crack cocaine to him. That dog would rather have a ball than breathe."

So would a dog named Blek.

★ ★ ★ 37 ★ ★ ★

THE SOUND OF BLEK SCREAMING

Military working dog Blek H199 didn't have much time between his fourth and fifth deployments. The black German shepherd returned to Maxwell Air Force Base in Alabama from Afghanistan in December 2009 with a handler who had bonded deeply with him. The two had found numerous explosives and grown to be best friends.

The handler would like to have stayed with six-year-old Blek for the rest of the dog's career. That was not to be.

In what's known as a "hot swap"—he had to give up Blek upon return from war, and Blek got a new handler, Air Force Staff Sergeant Brent Olson. He liked Blek immediately but felt a little guilty. "His other handler wouldn't even talk to me, he was so upset that I had his dog. They had really bonded. I was like, 'Dude, it's not my fault.'"

Less than three months later, Olson and Blek deployed to FOB Salerno/RC East and Kandahar/RC South, Afghanistan, where they were attached to the 101st Airborne, 502nd Bravo Company, Third Platoon. During their months there, they bonded over "all

193

that war stuff. We experienced firefights and we found IEDs and pretty much had a good time."

Like most military working dogs, Blek loved finding IEDs. He'd sniff and wag his tail hard and fast. "He'd be like, 'OK, Dad, I did good! Now give me my ball!'" Olson credits the predeployment training he and Blek got at Yuma a few months earlier with helping keep them safe, perhaps alive, during some tenuous moments. "We'd been through the dress rehearsal, so we were ready to perform."

They fought Taliban insurgents together for six months and spent almost every hour at each other's side. Life was about as good as it gets for a dog and handler at war, as far as Olson was concerned.

But on the night of September 16, 2010, through the odd green glow of night-vision goggles, Olson's war would take a dark turn.

It was the third night of a mission to clear a known hostile village in southern Afghanistan. Each day, as American and Afghan army troops swept buildings for insurgents, weapons, and caches, someone would open fire on them. It was a grueling mission. Troops were tired. But it was almost over. Just a few more buildings to go.

That night, after clearing three buildings, the platoon arrived at the fourth. It was near a huge marijuana field—a mud hut residence on the bottom, with stairs on the side leading up to a grape hut. Olson sent Blek up to check out the door frame to make sure it was not booby-trapped, and to sniff for IEDs on the mud stairs along the way. "Go up, boy!" Blek ran up, sniffed the twelve stairs, inspected around the bottom of the door frame with his nose, ran back down the stairs, and stood about ten feet away from Olson, awaiting his next command. Then an Afghan National Army (ANA) soldier ran up the stairs, followed within seconds by another Afghan soldier. They were going to open the hut and take a look at what lay inside. But when the second soldier got to the fourth step, there was a tremendous explosion.

What followed was a hellish scene.

A platoon sergeant got on the radio calling, "IED! IED!" The Afghan soldier who was on his way up the stairs was thrown twenty feet, onto an old dirt road. His left leg had been blown off, and he lay screaming, begging in Arabic for someone to shoot him. He quickly bled to death in the middle of the road.

The force of the explosion had blown Olson back a few feet into the wall behind him. He stood stunned. "What brought me back to reality was the sound of Blek screaming. It was a horrible sound."

He couldn't see his dog because it was nighttime, so he reeled Blek in on the retractable leash, pulling and pulling until Blek was next to him. Blek had run when the IED exploded, so the leash was out a good twenty-five feet. When he finally got him close, Olson was relieved that Blek was even alive. He felt his dog for any injuries. As he was running his hands up and down Blek's legs, Olson's right arm went completely numb. He put his left hand under his right armpit, and then drew it out—his hand was drenched with blood.

"I'm hit!" he yelled.

"Who's hit?"

"The dog handler!" Olson shouted back.

An army medic came over and started cutting off Olson's gear and clothing. Blek growled at the medic. "All he sees is someone touching me and me in pain, and he's like 'That's my dad. Leave him alone.'"

Olson couldn't take chances, and he handed off Blek to someone who was also hurt, but not completely out of the fight.

As the medic worked on Olson, the Afghan soldiers were running around in a panic. More IEDs went off as they ran into other buildings to seek shelter. The damaged platoon called in First Platoon for support because of all the casualties. As the troops ran in, they set off more IEDs. Two American soldiers died, and several others were wounded.

Olson had taken shrapnel to his right armpit, and his upper arm was broken and still devoid of feeling. His left arm was burned, shrapnel peppered his face, and he had a three-inch piece of metal in his leg.

He saw Blek again as they were waiting for a Black Hawk medevac. He knew right away that Blek had gone deaf. He was talking to his dog, but it was clear Blek could not hear him. The dog just stared straight ahead, panting. Blek's eardrums had been blown by the concussion. He also had a piece of shrapnel embedded in the left side of his muzzle.

Twenty minutes after the initial blast, the helicopter arrived.

"The dog can't go!" yelled a crewmember above the noise of the chopper.

"He has to go. If he doesn't go, I'm not going! There's no way I'm leaving my dog!"

Blek went with Olson on the Black Hawk to Kandahar. There, an ambulance sped Olson to the base hospital. Veterinary staffers took Blek to the vet hospital. "You're a good boy," Olson told him as they parted.

★

Two days later, Olson had a visitor at the hospital. Blek had come to see him, brought by another handler who was taking care of Blek. The dog jumped onto Olson's bed and just stared at him. "I almost cried." The dog's face was already better, but he was still deaf. Blek stayed with Olson for about a half hour and then went off on the first leg of his journey back to the States. They would meet up again briefly at Landstuhl Regional Medical Center in Germany.

Olson spent the next month going from one medical facility to the next. He had three surgeries, and one year later is back in fighting shape. He will be deploying to Afghanistan again in March 2012. This time he will not go with Blek. He is working Wiel R139, a young, high-strung Malinois fresh out of dog school. "I wish it were Blek, but he's a good dog. He's coming along pretty well."

As for Blek, he is now eight years old. He was deaf for two months and still has troubles with equilibrium from time to time because of his ear damage.

Olson has not forgotten his old comrade. In fact, he sees him every day. Blek is now officially Olson's dog. Blek couldn't work anymore because of his injury, and Olson jumped at the chance to adopt him. As a handler, he got first dibs.

Blek spends his days hanging out on the couch, sleeping in the comfort of a real bed, and eating dog treats shaped like prime rib bones. When he's not busy sleeping or eating, he follows Olson or his girlfriend around the house to see what they're up to. "He's my shadow," says Olson. "I'm going to miss him."

THE BUDDY SYSTEM

A true bond between soldiers is unparalleled, particularly a bond born in deployment. In part, because like a mother's bond with her child, you can't possibly explain it; it's too intense, it's unique—that closeness and camaraderie, the complete interdependence, and then of course the shared adrenaline rush during moments of life or death.

Every handler who has done it says that if you've never been a handler in a war situation, you'll never grasp it. You'll just never understand the razor-sharp dread and thrill of facing what's at stake together. You are absolutely dependent on that dog doing his thing. And the dog relies on you for everything else.

The dog is a check for what you might miss: the scent of an IED buried so cleverly there's no way to tell by looking, the sight of someone doing something that doesn't look quite right, the sound of an insurgent releasing a safety ever so quietly. And you're there to keep him out of the trouble he could wander into out of naïveté or enthusiasm.

How could you possibly explain the sensation of being

dependent upon such ability and, more so, surviving because of it? Who else would understand what that means and what it's like to owe your life to another creature—a creature that you could swear is humanly conscious in some way?

"The bond will pull you through the toughest situations," says Master Chief Scott Thompson, who was in charge of all dog-team operations for a year in Afghanistan. "I don't think there's anything else in the world that can compare to the bond between a handler and dog."

But as any dog lover knows, a bond can't be created overnight. It takes an investment of time, nurturing, and shared experiences. Sure, Jake will be enraptured with anyone who pays him the slightest attention. Once he even followed a jogger a mile down the beach before I could catch up with him and remind him of my existence. (The jogger had stopped to pet him, saying he was missing his own yellow Lab, who was back home in Connecticut; maybe Jake could sense the guy needed a pal.) But in the larger scheme of things, Jake and I have spent nine years together, and if he ever had to come to the defense of the jogger or me, I have no doubt he'd have my back.

It's the same with military working dogs. Initially, when a dog and handler are matched up, the goal is to establish a rapport. Blek had been with his previous handler for at least a year, and there were others before him, too. So Olson went out of his way to have long grooming sessions with the dog, to visit him more frequently than called for by protocol, to let him off leash in the fenced area to play catch. Blek was adaptable, outgoing, and willing to work, as long as he got his praise and his ball. It made for an easy transition.

But what about dogs who haven't had a handler before? What's it like to go from a breeder to a vendor to dog school to a kennel and finally get assigned a real handler?

★ ★ ★ 39 ★ ★ ★

THAT DOG WHO WAS
WALKING POINT

Fenji was young and green and needed a lot of fine-tuning when she was assigned to Corporal Max Donahue in February 2010 at Camp Pendleton. So it was up to Donahue to move her along to where she'd be ready for deployment.

He liked her enormously from the first time he met her. There was something about her happy demeanor, her eagerness to please. And he brought out the best in her, says his kennel master, Gunnery Sergeant Justin Green, "because he wasn't afraid to make a jackass of himself in front of his buddies. You have to be willing to put yourself out there and look like an idiot to look like gold to a dog." When Fenji performed a task successfully, there is no imitating the sound of the thrilled, goofy, crazy praise her handler lavished on his dog.

Like many other marines, Donahue had never been one to follow convention. He did things his way from the start. On July 14, 1987, his mom drove herself to the hospital between contractions because she'd gone into labor at 3 A.M., two weeks before she was due. Her husband was out of town, and "I didn't want to bother any friends just because my baby decided to make a grand appearance at a time of his choosing." Growing up, Donahue was always making grand appearances, it seems. He couldn't walk into a room without all eyes falling upon him. Something about his smile, his confident, congenial gait.

He got in plenty of trouble in his early years, fighting to defend his younger brother, disrupting class to tell a joke. As he got older, he drank, smoked, flirted, and got into more fights. But even as a rowdy teen, he'd always help someone who needed a hand. Broken down on the side of the road? He'd change your tire. ATM card not working at the gas station and you're out of gas? He'd fill your tank. Someone picking on a weaker kid? You'd be unwise to do that in front of Donahue.

As with many now serving in the military, September 11, 2001, was the day Donahue decided that he would join the armed forces when he was old enough. He told his mother, "I've decided: I'm going to become a marine and fight to protect this country."

He stayed true to his mission, and a month after he graduated from high school, he enlisted in the Marine Corps with the knowledge that he wanted to work with dogs. "To have a dog at your side while you fight for the good guys? A best friend right there to have your back and maybe save everyone around you?" he said. "It doesn't get any better than that."

★ ★ ★ 40 ★ ★ ★

SPECIAL EFFECTS

The effect these dogs have on their handlers can be profound. As army veterinarian Captain Emily Pieracci says, "You get these big burly guys and they melt with these dogs. They love them more than anything."

Everywhere you turn in the world of military working dogs, you will hear handlers trying to summarize how much their dogs mean to them: "My boss may be mad at me, my wife may be mad at me, but my dog is always happy to see me." "My biggest fear is of not getting assigned a dog and having to be a regular cop. It's like half of you is gone." "War would have been hell without my dog."

Air Force Staff Sergeant Chris Keilman was only eight months into being a handler when he got picked—he thinks totally at random—for a deployment with a Combined Joint Special Operations Task Force unit in Afghanistan. It took a while for this elite group to trust the new guy and his German shepherd, Kira L471. But after enough missions with the dog team out front—and

95 percent of the time, Kira led the way, with Keilman not far behind, and the others covering for him—they came to appreciate these two. They grew especially fond of the dog.

Keep in mind that these are tough warriors. They go on long missions in dangerous places and don't see a shower or outhouse for up to seventeen days at a time. There are no days off on these missions. They target insurgent leaders with great success. They go on missions about which I could not be told.

Kira's handler loves her and calls her "my girl," "my baby," "my sweetheart." (He is married, and his wife loves the dog, too.) "She was out there making sure we were safe every day. I would try to make her comfortable, massaging her belly, her pads. It wasn't much in return for what she did," he says.

But the effect this dog had on the rest of the troops is what's surprising. She would sit around the campfire with them as they ate, and they'd talk to her and pet her and reminisce about their own dogs. Kira was their number one morale booster on most days. And so, as Keilman puts it, "they babied the crap out of her."

"She got steak a lot when she was downrange. Anytime we'd get real meat, they were always giving her some. We'd be riding the RG (a mine-resistant light-armored vehicle), and Kira would stand in the front by the gunner, looking out the window. He'd feed her beef jerky the whole way.

"One of my guys, holy shit, he didn't like that she only had a duckboard to sleep on when she was in her crate. He was pissed that it was too hard. He went to the main FOB and bought her a memory foam pad. Someone else gave her a nice soft blanket."

★

Part of a dog's charm during deployment rests in the simple fact that the dog is friendly. Who better to tell your problems to than a dog? She won't tell anyone else, and she won't judge. Even just touching a dog, being around one, has been shown to have myriad health benefits, including lowering blood pressure and reducing stress levels.

"These dogs are there for you and will listen to you and will keep you company in what may be one of the worst places in the world. These dogs make your days over there a lot less lonely," says Thompson.

That accounts in part for why so many stray dogs in Afghanistan become an intimate part of the everyday lives of troops. "She'd just sit there with us the entire time, and if anyone wasn't doing well, she'd put her head on them and just close her eyes," Marine Corporal Ward Van Alstine told the *San Francisco Chronicle*, of Chloe, the stray he ended up adopting after his deployment. "She was the one thing that, no matter how bad the day was, she was our best friend."

A dog makes the most foreign situation seem a little more normal. Think about a time when you were in a new city or country, and you felt a little lost, a little upended. Then you saw a dog, and if you like dogs, you probably felt a bit more at home. If you got to make the dog's acquaintance, all the better.

Not all military working dogs can be good companions for the troops they're supporting. Some dual-purpose dogs are too unpredictable. What may seem like a friendly gesture to you—like reaching out your hand to pat a dog's head—could be interpreted as a threat. After all, these dogs have been trained to attack in certain situations when someone raises a hand. Some dogs can't tell the difference between those scenarios and what's intended as a friendly fireside ear rub.

But many dual-purpose dogs, and the vast majority of single-purpose dogs, provide a vital form of companionship on deployment. "Even if they're terrible at explosives, afraid of gunfire, and just have to sit around and color all day, a dog may do funny things that make time pass for everyone. It's comforting," says Gunny Knight.

The army even uses specially trained stress-therapy dogs, notably Labrador retrievers, to help deployed soldiers relax and cope better with the stresses they endure. Just by virtue of being their affable canine selves, these members of army combat stress teams can make a difference in how the rest of a soldier's deployment may go.

But the deepest levels of friendship are between dog and handler. They can be together almost 24/7 while deployed to remote areas with no kennels—and even on FOBs that have large kennel operations, if the handler chooses. More often than not, these dogs sleep in or near the handler's cot. Some dogs crawl right into their handler's sleeping bag; others curl up on the foot of the bed. Where there are no chow halls, they'll eat with the handler. Many even end up following their handlers into the shower.

Some will say that the best time in a soldier dog's life is during war. Instead of being with a handler only a few hours a day back home, and often not at all on weekends, in war they're almost inseparable.

"You know this dog so well, and he knows you," says Marine Sergeant Mark Vierig, whose story opened this part of the book. "Deployment seals it."

★ ★ ★ **41** ★ ★ ★

FOXHOLES

For more than a month in early 2011, Vierig slept in foxholes every night in the Upper Gereshk Valley of Afghanistan. Vierig and his combat tracker dog Lex were supporting the Third Battalion Eighth Marines Second Platoon, which was safeguarding the construction of the first paved road in the Helmand Province from Taliban attacks. As road construction moved on, so did they, and the marine found himself digging a new foxhole every few days.

It was a cold, wet time of year and rained heavily, daily, almost all day and all night long. Gore-Tex rain gear protected Vierig somewhat by day, and at night he'd take refuge in a sleeping bag in his muddy foxhole. The hole was like a shallow grave—about three feet deep, six feet long, and two feet wide. He also dug a connecting circular hole next to the part of his foxhole near his head. This was for Lex and his backpack. From the air, the whole setup would look like the letter P.

Every sopping night Vierig would sink into the foxhole to sleep and would get Lex in to bunk next to him to keep relatively dry.

He'd prop up his rifle under a camouflage tarp so the rain would run off and not flood their refuge. Rocks kept the outside of the tarp in place. Every night Vierig would wake up at least a couple of times to scoop water from a deep hole he'd dug at the foot to collect water so his foxhole wouldn't flood.

But when Vierig awoke in the middle of the night, Lex was rarely in the foxhole. It was baffling the first time it happened, but the marine raised the tarp and looked outside and found his dog. This would go on every night during those wet weeks. "He'd just be standing there, in the rain, just standing guard over me." The dog did not sit, but stood, head erect, large triangular ears at attention and focused for sounds, eyes peering into the darkness for any sign of intrusion. His coat was soaked with rain, but he stood riveted, noble.

"I'd tell him, 'Hey you, come on in here!'" and the dog would leave his post and go to his subterranean room—at least until Vierig fell asleep again. When Vierig would wake up a couple of hours later ready to scoop more rain with his empty half-plastic water bottle, Lex would be back up on volunteer duty.

Did Lex sleep during this time? "I wondered that a lot. I asked him 'When do you sleep, dog?' He spent a lot of sleepless nights watching over me."

As Lex protected Vierig, so Vierig protected Lex. "Would I sacrifice another human life to save him? I would not. But I'd do everything in my power to save him." It's a common refrain among military working dogs handlers. The Department of Defense may officially consider military working dogs to be equipment, but most handlers—while they know that's the bottom line—see things quite differently. "My rifle is a piece of equipment," says Vierig. "But I don't feel the same about my rifle as I do about my dog."

One day during their month of foxholes, Vierig and Lex joined another platoon for a short mission. Everyone else had already dug in, but Vierig was a newcomer, so he got to work digging his foxhole into a barren, rocky hill. It was the full six feet long but barely over a foot deep when insurgents fired an 82mm heavy recoilless rifle in his direction. The explosive round hit thirty feet from Vierig, although it was likely aimed at a nearby tank.

Without thinking, Vierig grabbed Lex by the scruff of his neck and threw him into the foxhole. Then he jumped down and covered Lex's body so the dog wouldn't get hit. Most of Vierig's body protruded from the semi-dug foxhole, but he had his flak and Kevlar and figured he was a lot less vulnerable out in the open than Lex would have been.

Suddenly another explosion rocked the earth just fifteen feet away. Lex remained calm under Vierig. "When stuff goes down in a situation like that, dogs know what's going on. They're like, 'OK, this is serious.'"

Then out of nowhere, man and dog started laughing. It's incongruous, Vierig knows, but it's the only way he can describe it. There they were, face-to-face, nose-to-nose almost, in this vastly dangerous situation, and Lex gave Vierig a look that seemed to say, "This is a most ridiculous position we're in, don't you think?" If you had been an insurgent and you saw this up close, you would have thought they were going a bit mad. As a former professional bull rider, Vierig has laughed in the face of danger before. "But it's a lot better when you're with your dog."

★ ★ ★ 42 ★ ★ ★

REX . . . AND CINTE

In civilian life, the idea is that you stay with your dog until death do you part. Unfortunately, too many people don't, which is why shelters are so overcrowded, but that's another story.

By contrast, in military life, handlers play a game of musical canines. They get assigned a dog for a set period—a deployment, a year, a few years, depending on their specialty and the luck of the draw—but it's generally not a pairing that lasts a dog's career. Handlers switch dogs, dogs switch handlers, all depending on the jobs that must be done.

Kennel masters often try to match dog to handler, but sometimes a handler gets stuck with whatever dog happens to be around and available, and the match can be downright dreadful. Some pairings stay that way for the duration. But as any dog lover can attest to, dogs have their ways of working themselves into people's hearts. Military dogs are no exception.

When Army Sergeant Amanda Ingraham learned she had been assigned to work with Rex L274 in 2008, she was aghast. "Of all the dogs, why him?" she wondered.

The army had tried to pair the four-year-old German shepherd with other handlers, but no one could work with him. You had to yell to get him to do anything. He chased everything that moved, from wild mules in Arizona to rabbits in Texas to squirrels in Virginia. Being a specialized search dog (SSD), he worked off leash, and chasing critters while looking for IEDs was not an option.

But Ingraham seemed to be the only person the dog would listen to even remotely while training. For instance, once during night training, Rex was doing nothing she asked, and in frustration she yelled, "Good God, you can't even *sit*!" And he sat. It was a rare command that he would obey. Another time, she told him to come to her. He was on a footbridge twelve feet above her. Most normal dogs would run off a footbridge to get to their handler. Not Rex. He jumped straight down twelve feet to his sergeant.

The man in charge said the dog was hers.

Specialized search dogs stay with a handler longer than most other dogs stay with their handlers. Stints of four or five years together are not uncommon. After spending a couple of months with Rex, Ingraham was counting the days until her contract with the army was up, especially after the dog led her dangerously close to faux explosives. And more than once. "I'd be right on top of it by the time I saw it. He showed no change of behavior like he's supposed to. I'd have been dead if it were the real deal." She was almost certain she would not reenlist in eighteen months. She couldn't bear the thought of spending more time with this wretched dog.

The two eventually headed to Yuma Proving Ground for predeployment training. They were to go to Iraq together. The thought made Ingraham queasy.

One day Rex once again led her right on top of an IED, and she was yelling at him, pushing him on to sniff out more and do it right. He refused to do anything. He just sat there, as if on strike. "I was yelling as much as I could yell. I said, 'What's the matter with you? You want me to ask you *nicely?*'" She has no idea where the words came from. The very notion struck her as ridiculous, since he had never responded to anything but yelling.

But she gave her next command in the kind of polite tone you reserve for speaking with people who are listening. "Rex, get on," she told him, which meant for him to go out away from her and search. He did just what she asked. "Get over," and he'd go left or right, depending on her arm signal. "This way!" and he came bounding back to her. She was shocked. Thrilled. He looked proud. From then on, she would rarely have to raise her voice again. They had come to a meeting of minds. Whether handler broke through to dog or dog broke through to handler didn't matter. There was common ground. They were starting to speak the same language.

That night, Ingraham let Rex sleep on her bed in the hotel. She'd heard it was good for creating a bond, but she'd never felt like letting the big beast up there. Rex weighed ninety-six pounds. (Ingraham often wondered how she would manage to lift him over her shoulder, as handlers sometimes have to do downrange.) It was the first time anyone had offered Rex such a privilege. He didn't know much about beds. He fell out of bed almost immediately. He decided that sleeping crossways was a safer option, and Ingraham couldn't budge him. So she joined him, head on one side of the bed, feet at the other.

"The next day, he was like a brand-new dog," she says. That day Rex was the star of the school. He went hundreds of meters from

Ingraham during one exercise and gave a big enough change of behavior that she could see what he was doing. Instead of barely showing a subtle tail movement, he wagged hard when he found the explosive. She didn't have to yell at him once. No one could believe it was the same dog.

In a few weeks they deployed to Iraq, supporting various units and missions over the coming months. Rex's nose was strong and his drive to sniff out explosives stronger. Units frequently requested his help because he was such a good worker, and also because he was big and not the traditional breed of dog that works as a specialized search dog. Those are usually sporting breeds, like Labs, since the job doesn't require a biting dog, just a good sniffer.

Enemy soldiers aren't terribly scared of Labs, and for good reason. Around the world they're seen as the friendly dogs they generally are. Some Labs might do serious damage if a handler were in trouble, but these dogs don't have the ferocious reputation German shepherds and Malinois do. To have a huge shepherd like Rex doing the job of a Lab just added to his popularity among the platoons. Just the sight of him might send the bad guys running.

But what insurgents didn't know was that as big and scary as Rex looked, he was a gentle giant. He had failed out of aggression training at Lackland because anytime he bit someone wearing protective gear during practice, and they yelled or screamed in response, he immediately let go and seemed to look concerned and sad. You could imagine him saying, "Sorry, mate. I thought we were just having a bit of fun. I hope you're going to be all right." Nevertheless, when he broke off a tooth during an aggression exercise, the vet replaced it with a glistening titanium one.

But gradually people at Lackland realized this dog was about as aggressive as a deer. "The only thing he used that titanium tooth for was eating his food," says Ingraham.

Rex's sensitivity made him an informal therapy dog for deployed troops. "He'd always find the one soldier who was having a hard day and hang out with them," says Ingraham. But his favorite therapy was to cheer up down soldiers by getting them to play with a water bottle. After all, he liked playing with water bottles, so it would seem natural that others would, too. He'd run up and bonk the soldier with a water bottle (empty or full, it didn't matter). Or he'd sit next to him crunching the bottle and periodically banging it against the soldier who was blue or scared. Eventually the soldier would take the bait, and a grand game of tug-of-war or a big chase would ensue.

Rex's sensitivity also proved helpful in scouting work—something he came by accidentally. One day Rex was with a platoon in a field with grass much taller than his head, and he was sniffing for explosives. Ingraham and the other soldiers got information from a drone above that someone was hiding in the field. A few minutes later, Rex yelped and ran back to Ingraham. It was a behavior she had seen during training, when someone had hidden and startled him. She knew that same thing had just happened in the tall grass. "I was able to tell a couple of people with me where the man was in front of us and how many steps to the left or right he was." They apprehended him, and Rex got a tennis ball. Another time he sniffed at something in a barn the same way and looked at Ingraham with such a scared expression that she knew there was someone hiding under the hay.

It wasn't heroic, but it got the job done.

But gentle as he was, he would have killed for Ingraham. She was climbing out of a ravine when she lost her footing and fell to the ground. An Iraqi interpreter reached down to help her and was leaning down close to her. Rex took this the wrong way and charged the man, growling and barking ferociously. Ingraham was able to call off Rex before he did any harm. Rex would even stand guard at the shower trailer, barking protectively while she was in there.

She credits their successes on missions and on base to knowing each other so well. "We wouldn't have been able to do half of what we did without the bond. I knew almost every move he made. I could read almost every emotion in his face. You learn to read everything, and they learn to read everything about you. It got to the point where if I sat, he sat. If I lay down, he lay down."

Rex was still a stubborn dog with others. He wouldn't take commands from anyone else, no matter how nicely they asked or how much they coerced. He was a one-handler dog. "Sometimes if someone told him to do something and he was with me, he'd just open his mouth and wag his tail and look back at me like he was laughing at them."

While deployed, Rex and Ingraham were together day in, day out. He spent nights on her bed, or on an extra bunk next to her, or curled up on some bedding below her bed. During the day, if she happened to be working at a desk while at FOB Warhorse (one of the better living conditions during their deployment), Rex would sleep on a giraffe bed Ingraham had bought online. Rex is probably the only deployed dog who ever slept on a dog bed with a giraffe print and a squeaky giraffe-shaped head sticking out of the top. He liked to play with its head for awhile, chomping it to make it squeak, until he got tired and plopped down for a good nap.

Every night before bedtime, Ingraham would lean down close

to her dog and tell him, "I love you, Rex. Everything from your big feet to your stinky breath." And he'd drift off to sleep.

Early in their deployment, Ingraham decided that she would reenlist. If all went well, she would be able to retire at about the same time Rex would be retiring, after a couple more rotations together in Afghanistan. "I would adopt him and he was going to live on my couch in Waverly, West Virginia." It was a perfect plan.

Their Iraq deployment done, they went back to the States, where they were stationed once again at Fort Myer, a small army base next to the Arlington National Cemetery in Virginia. It was very hard for Ingraham to leave Rex back in the kennels every night. She provided him with a dog bed (something most dogs don't get, partly because so many would chew it up) and visited him frequently, even on days off.

While there, they went on some presidential missions together, making sure the coast was clear for the chief executive and his entourage. At one event at Fort Myer, scores of wounded warrior soldiers and veterans showed up. It was one of those times Ingraham realized what a special dog she had.

Although the dogs don't search people at these events, any wheelchairs have to be searched, because they can't go through scanners. "It's sensitive, because you know what they've been through." Of the three dogs present, Rex was chosen for the duty because of his gentle nature.

"The first wheelchair came in, and instead of searching, Rex just walked up to the man sitting in it and laid his head on the

Lex L479 and his handler would go to sleep in the foxholes they shared while on patrol in Afghanistan. Soon after his handler fell asleep, the Belgian Malinois would crawl out from their tarp-protected foxhole and stand guard over him through the night—often in torrential rains. MARINE SERGEANT MARK VIERIG

Marine Corporal Max Donahue and Fenji M675—shown here in Garmsir, Afghanistan—bonded as soon as they met at Camp Pendleton, San Diego, six months earlier. MARINE GUNNERY SERGEANT CHRIS WILLINGHAM

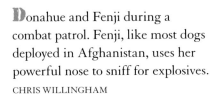

Donahue and Fenji during a combat patrol. Fenji, like most dogs deployed in Afghanistan, uses her powerful nose to sniff for explosives. CHRIS WILLINGHAM

Donahue and Fenji on patrol in a marketplace in Garmsir. "You asked if Fenji has a good nose," says Marine Gunnery Sergeant Chris Willingham, who took this photo. "I wouldn't have been walking behind her if she didn't." CHRIS WILLINGHAM

Air Force Staff Sergeant Brent Olson was awarded a Purple Heart for his actions in Afghanistan. Blek, who was also injured, received nothing. Military working dogs do not officially get commendations. "Dogs are soldiers, too. They give up their whole lives for this," says Olson. "Not to be recognized officially is a slap in the face." U.S. ARMY PHOTO BY SERGEANT JEFFREY ALEXANDER

Olson and Blek on a mountain mission in Afghanistan. U.S. ARMY PHOTO BY SERGEANT JEFFREY ALEXANDER

"He always had my back," says Air Force Staff Sergeant James Bailey, of his first military working dog, Robby D131. He has since adopted Robby.
JAMES BAILEY

Rex L274 on guard in Iraq as his soldiers take a lunch break in their Stryker vehicle. Rex did not make it as a patrol dog because he was too gentle. "If you were playing and you acted as if he bit you, he'd let go and look all sad," Army Sergeant Amanda Ingraham says. But she knew he would put his life on the line to protect her. AMANDA INGRAHAM

Ingraham on a mission with Rex in Iraq. More than anything, she remembers the companionship he provided her and the other troops. "He'd always find the one soldier who was having a hard day and hang out with them." AMANDA INGRAHAM

Marine Sergeant Mark Vierig and Lex L479, on patrol in Afghanistan's Upper Gereshk Valley during rainy season. A common refrain among handlers who have deployed: "War would have been hell without my dog." MARK VIERIG.

Army Staff Sergeant Marcus Bates enjoys a little down time with Davy. MARCUS BATES

Air Force Staff Sergeant Christine Campos relaxes on her cot with her dog, Bico F544. Dogs on deployment often share their handlers' bunks and even sleeping bags. Being together nearly 24/7 deepens the bond between dog and handler. CHRISTINE CAMPOS

Ajax L523 shows off his pearly whites after his handler, Air Force Staff Sergeant James Bailey, gave them a good brushing while on deployment. JAMES BAILEY

War hero Fenji needs to wear "Doggles" to help with an eye problem, but she doesn't much care for them. When she's not working, she tries to take them off at every opportunity. MARIA GOODAVAGE

Marine dog handlers mourn the loss of a beloved fellow handler—one who appears in this book. MARINE PHOTO BY CORPORAL SKYLER TOOKER

man's lap and looked up to him." Ingraham realized this was Rex's way of signaling to her that there was nothing to worry about with this one. After Ingraham assured the soldier the dog was friendly, he gave Rex a pat on the head and moved on. This happened with every person who came in a wheelchair. Rex even gave soldiers on crutches special attention, but essentially ignored the uninjured. "He knew the wounded warriors. As always with him, he seemed to sense who needed the most care. I was so proud watching him."

In early 2011 Ingraham got word that they would be heading to Germany for a few months, with the idea that a deployment to Afghanistan would follow. She was excited that soon she'd be able to spend 24/7 with Rex again, even if meant their lives would be at stake with every step they took outside the wire.

But on March 16 she went to check on him in his kennel and right away she noticed something was amiss. There was foam in his water bowl and the dog didn't look right. She took him outside, where he passed up a chance to eat food, which was not like him. He made efforts to go to the bathroom, but he couldn't. She let him off leash, and instead of running exuberantly, he lay down by the fence. She took his tennis ball and threw it down the field, but he didn't move. She began to realize that something was terribly wrong.

She took the dog straight to the vet, where he was given several tests and screenings, including X-rays and ultrasound. Blood work was done. Everything came back OK.

They returned to the kennel, where she watched him all night.

"I tried not to panic, because he picks up on everything I do." Around 9 A.M. his heart rate jumped, and he started throwing up. The vets, who had left base, came back for him. They did all the tests again and still couldn't see anything. The vet called several different vets in the area, and they decided to send Rex to Fort Belvoir, about forty minutes away. There was a surgeon there. More tests there, same results. The surgeon said, "Let's go in and see what's going on inside."

Ingraham opted to stay in the room with her dog. "You'd rather see everything that happens to your dog." She could read the vet's face before the vet said anything. Something had twisted deep inside of Rex, and his colon was gray, essentially dead. The vet worked tirelessly to save Ingraham's dog, but in the end, there was nothing more he could do. (A military veterinarian I described Rex's condition to said it was not bloat, but likely a very rare, fatal condition called mesenteric root torsion.)

The veterinarian decided at that point that Rex would not come out of his anesthesia. Ingraham burst into tears. The vet administered the dose of euthanasia solution. Everyone left the room so Ingraham could be alone with him. She tried to keep it together, for his sake. She kissed him, stroked his head, and talked to him like old times.

Then she leaned down, snuggled into his fur, and told him, "I love you, Rex. Everything from your big feet to your stinky breath."

And he drifted off.

Less than a month later, and still raw from the loss of Rex, Ingraham learned that the army had assigned her to work with a new dog, Cinte M401. She was aghast. "Of all the dogs, why him?" she once again wondered.

She had seen the Belgian Malinois in the kennels and had been grateful he was not her dog. The four-year-old dog was clearly slow on the uptake. Much to Ingraham's dismay, he bonded with her almost immediately, following her around and always wanting to nuzzle up to her. But she didn't want him touching her. She was still aching from losing Rex. And besides, this dog was just annoying.

Her mother said to give it time, said she thought this sounded like a nice dog, but Ingraham knew she'd never like this dog.

In autumn of 2011, when we last communicated, Ingraham and Cinte had been in Germany for a couple of months. And as her mother predicted, Cinte was starting to grow on Ingraham. "His quirkiness has found a place in my heart."

Here's what she wrote me about this dog:

"He's a bit skittish so everyday noise is a challenge full of new things for him. For example, he was searching a box and he touched it and it moved, so he jumped like a cat onto a cart next to him as if he'd never seen a box move before.

"As he searches, every time he finds what he's looking for he gets this shocked look on his face that seems to say, 'OMG did you know that was there?' Also he tends to overthink things as simple as a command of sit.

"Then, there are children. He is terrified to the core. Even if the children are at a distance he will hide behind me or try to run as far away from them as he can, often without looking where he is going and running into anything in his path. He is a challenge but every day holds new surprises and it's never dull.

"Cinte is very clumsy and careless when he runs or fetches his toy and has repeatedly smashed his snout, so we are looking to make sure some of his issues aren't medical. He's a great dog and knows his job and loves doing it, but he seems to have a harder time doing it when compared to the other working dogs. His nose is weaker than any of his breed we have seen, but he seems to know and works harder. In a deployment situation I would trust him; he has no problems finding the mass odors of IEDs and other caches, but he may miss a single magazine of ammo.

"It may be a while before we are proficient enough to go to Afghanistan, but when we go, it will be a good deployment."

★ ★ ★ **43** ★ ★ ★

ALWAYS AROUND

The kind of tender relationship Ingraham and Rex developed, and the kind that seems to be blossoming with her and Cinte, is not unique to this war.

Robert Kollar was a handler with the Fifty-eighth Infantry Platoon Scout Dog Unit in Vietnam, during 1968–69. He was based at Camp Evans and given a German shepherd named Rebel. According to the Vietnam Dog Handler Association, there were fifty-two dogs named Rebel who served in Vietnam. Few fates are known, but at least five were killed in action, four were put down because of their injuries, one retired, and one died of heat stress. That was Kollar's dog, who died three weeks after Kollar, who was a sergeant, returned home.

He remembers so vividly when he and Rebel would be dropped off to walk around the jungle for five days at a time, walking point, and how it seemed like you were always assigned to a unit where you didn't know anybody. You're on the point in front of strangers, and so in all senses it's just you and the dog. In the monsoon season and the dead heat of summer. On good days and bad—like the night

Kollar was part of a night ambush, but he could not keep Rebel up. The dog just would not stay awake, and Kollar had to keep pulling him up to keep watch. It's all about teamwork, of course, but in this kind of work the team is less you and the patrol, more you and the one other soul in the world who, after weeks or months together, understands who you are and what this is all about, and that when you put on the scouting harness the real game is about to begin.

"With Rebel I was always going to his hooch," Kollar remembers. "What a sweet dog. A real pussycat. Not aggressive at all, but then he didn't need to be. I was always going to see how he was doing; I'd sit with him, talk to him, we'd listen to the audiocassettes from home. He was my main man. I don't know how else to tell you. A dog like that is a real friend; it's also the one link you have with home."

In between patrols, which might last for days, Kollar would work with the dog constantly, to keep him tuned, to keep the game going. They would practice basic obedience and hand signals, and they might go down the "training lane" to see what had been planted, to keep the dog razor-sharp. Kollar found the ritual of taking care of the dog each day helpful and morale-boosting.

It's been forty-three years since Kollar worked with Rebel, but he's never forgotten it, and of the fifty or so photos and mementos hanging on the walls of his bedroom, eight or nine show Rebel. And Kollar's got his collar and choke chain mounted.

For Kollar, "Rebel is always around."

He likes to point out the photos of him and Rebel that appear on Michael Lemish's Web site, k9writer.com. One page features photos of handlers and their dogs from different wars.

Kollar's favorite photo from that collection is not from Vietnam but rather a photo taken during World War II, at battle of Peleliu, which is sometimes called "the bitterest battle of the war for the marines." Fought in the fall of 1944, the battle's casualties were among the highest of any Pacific War battle. Eight marines from the battle were given the Medal of Honor—five posthumously. Some of the fighting was hand-to-hand, throwing whatever you had at the enemy. And all to take an island with dubious military value.

The photo is of a young marine from the Fifth Marine War Dog Platoon, Corporal William Scott, and his Doberman pinscher, Prince, in what looks like a foxhole on the beach. The soldier is on his knees, rifle in his right hand, left hand on the dog's shoulder. The soldier is looking up and not at the camera. It is not an unusual photo. Others on Lemish's site are more interesting or just better quality photos, but for some reason, for Kollar this photo catches everything one might say about being a handler. But he cannot explain it, even to his wife.

If there is a key to the appeal, perhaps it's the soldier's expression, blank at first glance, but look at it for a moment and you see fatigue and also confidence. A brashness even. And then it all becomes a little clearer. Look at the photo for what it implies: a soldier and his dog and nothing else, beyond all other identities, alone, the two of them against the world.

The history of dogs in relation to war is almost entirely about how dogs have been used for thousands of years to protect, detect, or attack, and about the glory or terror dogs bring to the fight. The bond that makes this all possible is implied but rarely described.

But if you look beyond traditional tales of war, in the footnotes of famous battles, you can get an interesting perspective on the importance of this bond. Two of my favorite stories are not about war dogs, per se, but about the effect that a dog found on a battlefield had on renowned military leaders.

George Washington, whose many canines included hunting dogs by the name of Sweet Lips, Venus, Truelove, Taster, Tippler, and Drunkard, understood the emotional bond between dogs and their owners. Dogs were both his passion and his hobby.

During the Battle of Germantown in October 1777, when things were not going well for the Americans, a little terrier was found wandering between American and British lines. A check of his collar revealed him to be the dog of British General William Howe. He had somehow become lost on the battlefield.

Against the desires of some soldiers who wanted to keep the dog as a spoil, or to weaken Howe's resolve, Washington ordered a cease-fire. An aide wrote this note and attached it to the dog's collar: "General Washington's compliments to General Howe. He does himself the pleasure to return him a dog, which accidentally fell into his hands, and by the inscription on the Collar appears to belong to General Howe."

The shooting stopped on both sides, and under a flag of truce, Washington's aides brought the little dog back to his rightful owner. In some versions of the story, Howe was so impressed by Washington's honor that he began to take a more compassionate view of colonists, and eventually resigned his post.

Napoléon Bonaparte had a similar experience. The famously hard-hearted military leader was brought to tears as he inspected the battlefield after the Battle of Castiglione in 1796. He came across a dog mourning a dead soldier. The loyal dog sat by the soldier's corpse after everyone else had fled. He was groaning and licking the soldier's hand, then trying to draw Napoléon to the soldier's side.

The scene deeply affected the emperor, who wrote about it during his long exile:

> *No occurrence of any of my other battlefields impressed me so keenly. I halted on my tour to gaze at the spectacle and reflect on its meaning. . . . This soldier, I realized, must have had friends at home and in his regiment; yet he lay there deserted by all except his dog. . . . I had looked on, unmoved, at battles, which decided the future of nations. Tearless, I had given orders which brought death to thousands. Yet here I was stirred, profoundly stirred, stirred to tears. And by what? The grief of one dog.*

★ ★ ★ **44** ★ ★ ★

BEYOND DEATH

In Afghanistan, war-related deaths are an everyday occurrence. Those of us not directly involved with the military read about the numbers, the names, the condensed stories of a too-short life, and we shake our heads, we feel the sting of another tragic loss, or many losses, and maybe we think about the families back home and how their lives are forever changed. And then we move on, our day perhaps a bit heavier. After years of this, the names and stories tend to blend together, and it's hard to remember what or where or especially why.

But when a soldier dog is involved, when news media come out with details of a dog being any part of a fight, especially one that ends in tragedy, for some reason the story is not easily forgotten.

I have met people who know little about what's going on in Afghanistan, but who can tell you months after it happened about the soldier dog who died, or the dog who protected his best friend to the end. It doesn't mean these people don't care about the countless men and women making the ultimate sacrifice. There's just something about these soldier dogs and their loyalty and devotion. . . .

Explosives-detection dog Eli, a black Labrador retriever, was a vital part of his handler's life, both on and off patrol in Afghanistan. Marine Private First Class Colton Rusk shared meals and his cot with the dog. Eli liked to stretch out when he slept, and the dog would often end up with more of the cot than Rusk.

Rusk didn't mind at all. "Whatever is mine is his," he wrote on his Facebook page. When he called home to talk to his family, it was always about Eli. When he sent pictures, the dog was inevitably in them. It made his mother feel better knowing her twenty-year-old son wasn't alone.

On December 6, 2010, they were on a mission in Sangin, in the Helmand Province—one of the most deadly areas in the region at that point. Eli had already sniffed out two explosives. It was looking like a good mission for the team.

But then there was a firefight. Rusk went down. Eli ran over to him. According to marine accounts, the dog crawled on top of Rusk in what could only be interpreted as an attempt to protect him. He snapped at other marines who ran over to move Rusk away from the battle, and even bit one of them.

This Labrador retriever, who had become such an essential part of Rusk's life, did not want to give him up so easily in death.

In Rusk's obituary, Eli was listed first among his survivors.

A true bond knows no direction. A dog loves his handler who loves his dog, back and forth and on and on. A dog helps his dying handler. A handler helps his dying dog. The lyrics may be different but the melody is the same.

About two weeks after Rusk died, Marine Lance Corporal William "Billy" Crouse IV was on patrol with his chocolate Lab, a bomb-detection dog named Cane. They were looking for IEDs along a roadway so others could follow safely. An IED found them first.

A helicopter rushed in. As Crouse was being evacuated, he cried out, "Get Cane in the Black Hawk!" Then he lost consciousness.

They were his last words.

His dog, terribly wounded, died as well.

At an auditorium at Lackland Air Force Base—the same auditorium where new handlers graduate from the dog program—memorial plaques for Rusk and Crouse hang side by side, in order of their deaths, in a row of plaques honoring fallen handlers. They are no longer at the end of the row.

You look at the row and find yourself trying not to wonder who will fill the next space. Will any of the men and women who are picking up their diplomas right now on the stage end up on this wall? You can't think about that. It's not right. They look so thrilled to be starting their careers as soldier dog handlers. You don't go there.

So you switch to a better track. Who will their dogs be? What kinds of bonds will they form? Will their dogs nestle into their sleeping bags on frigid nights at their patrol bases and keep them safe against those who would do them harm? Will the handlers survive, physically and mentally? How about their dogs?

★ ★ ★ 45 ★ ★ ★

AFTER THE TRAUMATIC STRESS

I'm walking down the aisle between two long rows of kennels at Lackland Air Force Base's adoption kennels. The dogs, as always seems to be the case at large kennels, are going nuts. The cacophony of excited barks makes me wish I'd taken up someone's offer of earplugs before we entered. Several dogs are spinning in fast circles like whirling dervishes. Others run back and forth. And then I come to Buck P027.

Buck is a chocolate Lab. Labs are normally rambunctious, happy dogs, and I would have expected him to be woofing with the rest. But he is curled up in a tight ball toward the back of his kennel. He seems like the only normal, calm one among these superenergetic dogs. But there is something about his eyes, his demeanor, that seems almost sad. He doesn't lift his head; he just looks at me unblinkingly, and then stares out again, eyes not seeming to focus on anything much.

Buck, it turns out, was in Afghanistan as a marine IED detector dog (IDD). The man taking me through the kennels tells me, "He heard one too many explosions." Buck has been diagnosed with canine post-traumatic stress disorder. He did not respond well enough to treatment, so tomorrow he will be picked up by thrilled new owners and given a new life as a civilian dog.

Months after I met poor Buck, his new people, Larry Sargent and his wife, Lynette, updated me on how he's doing. "We love him to death, and we're seeing his inner puppy a lot the way he plays," says Larry, a San Antonio pastor. "But we still have a lot we're trying to figure out about him." Buck is pretty clingy with him and needs to be attached to him by a leash when people come by, or the dog gets too nervous. And once, on a visit to the veterinary hospital at Lackland, Buck "completely froze" when he saw some soldiers in uniform. "He just lay down. He wouldn't even take treats from them," he says. Only after they walked past did Buck move again.

The Sargents wonder if it brought back memories of war—or perhaps worse yet, if Buck thought maybe his days of happiness on his quiet acre of land with this doting couple were over, and that he was going back to war. "It's a heartbreaking thought," says Lynette.

Until early 2011, PTSD was not officially recognized in dogs. A few years earlier, veterinarian Walter Burghardt, chief of behavioral medicine and military working dog studies at Lackland's Daniel E. Holland Military Working Dog Hospital, had seen a number of dogs come back from deployment with what looked like clear signs of PTSD. He and colleague Kelly Mann, a veterinary radiologist and director of the veterinary hospital, developed a survey for handlers to track possible signs of PTSD. For the next two years they collected data and weeded out dogs with preexisting issues, like fear of thunderstorms, or post-event problems, like short-term anxiety.

The result: About 5 percent of dogs were coming back with signs of what they could diagnose as PTSD.

Burghardt held a blue-ribbon panel meeting in January 2011 to see if nearly three dozen top experts and researchers could come to a conclusion about whether or not canine PTSD exists. The result was a consensus statement that some dogs do, indeed, qualify for the diagnosis.

Panel members weighed in on whether to use the term *PTSD*, because it might be considered an affront to people who have served their country and been diagnosed with the syndrome themselves. It was decided to officially call it canine PTSD to at least partially mitigate the issue.

Signs of canine PTSD include hypervigilance, increased startle response, attempts to run away or escape, withdrawal, changes in rapport with a handler, and problems performing trained tasks— like a bomb dog who just can't focus on sniffing out bombs anymore. These are variations of PTSD's symptoms in humans.

Burghardt points out a misnomer in one piece of the name PTSD: the word *stress*. "It's more *di*stress; stress that can't be mediated." And as with PTSD, the causes of the canine version are highly variable. What may result in problems in one individual may not affect another at all. Just as different people react to events in different ways, some dogs shrug off what could shut others down.

Sporting breeds, like Labs, appear to be more prone to PTSD than traditional dual-purpose dogs, like German shepherds and Malinois. Burghardt is not sure of the reasons, but he and Mann and a small team at Lackland are starting to investigate this and dozens of other questions about the disorder, including how to prevent it and how to best treat it. Right now, affected dogs are given time off and get a combination of drugs and different therapies. A dog who is shaking and hiding may be given antianxiety medication; one who is withdrawn could get antidepressants.

The success rate is not great so far. About one-fourth of soldier dogs being treated go back to their jobs. One-fourth are assigned to less stressful jobs, in which deployment is likely out of the question. Another fourth need long-term therapy, from three to six months.

About 25 percent will not be able to work again and end up being retired from service. Depending on their condition, they could go to a police force or be adopted by a family or an individual, as Buck has been.

Burghardt and Mann are studying dogs like Buck to investigate what can go wrong inside a dog. They're also looking at dogs who face unthinkably violent and terrifying conditions and are able to return to service with a bounce in their step.

Dogs in horrendous situations . . . As Burghardt describes the hell some dogs have been through, I think about Fenji. . . .

$$\star \; \star \; \star \quad \mathbf{46} \quad \star \; \star \; \star$$

SEMPER FIDELIS

Marine Sergeant Rosendo Mesa immediately looks up toward his EOD partner when he hears the explosion. He's afraid of what he will see. Only last week an IED detonated on another EOD partner as he was defusing it.

But when Mesa looks toward the other tech, who is working on the first of four IEDs Fenji has alerted to this morning, he's fine. Then they both see it; a rising billow of dark smoke a hundred meters away. It's coming from where they had last seen Corporal Max Donahue. He had been lying down, rifle poised, ready to engage against an ambush if needed. Fenji had been lying just a few feet away, attached to him by her leash.

One of the roles of an EOD tech is to run to an explosion where there may be an injury, give emergency care to any victims, and investigate the IED. The other marines stay put, ready to fire, to protect the mission and the EOD techs. Mesa and his partner sprint toward the smoke. There's a hole where Donahue had been keeping watch. Fenji is lying near it, bleeding from her ears, unable to get up.

They find Donahue ten meters from the blast hole. He's on his back, in a pool of blood, left leg gone at the thigh, right leg missing below the knee. He's blinking, but Mesa doesn't think he knows what hit him. Mesa has seen years of blast injuries, and it's not just the fireball that tears people up, it's the earthquake in the skull. The air itself becomes like shrapnel. And sure the vest takes the brunt, but you're talking about ten pounds of ammonium nitrate and aluminum, encased in a metal container planted a foot deep in the ground.

Donahue had been lying right on top of the bomb. It had been the perfect lookout spot. And it wasn't by chance that this bomb went off. While the other EOD tech works on Donahue, Mesa finds a cord leading from the IED to about two hundred meters south, to a small village. The cord is roughly hidden under dirt. He doesn't follow it all the way. He knows enough. This is what's called a command wire IED. All the enemy on the other end had to do was wait for a good opportunity and put a battery to the cord.

Even the best marine, the best dog, can't always catch these things. Instinct fails. Or there just aren't enough atoms floating above the dirt to detect. Or maybe somebody was tired, or assumed something. It happens. It's nobody's fault.

Just as the EOD techs get the tourniquets on Donahue and the major bleeding stops, the marines start taking fire. The two men quickly lift Donahue between them, like you would if a friend had twisted his ankle. They just grip him for life and run. They run down the dirt road in the 117-degree heat with bullets flying at them, as the other marines fire on their assailants. The corpsman (a medic everyone calls "Doc") follows them, and in about three hundred meters they come to a place on a tributary of the Helmand River where they can cross. They set Donahue down, and the corpsman tends to severe wounds on his abdomen, where even his body armor couldn't completely protect him.

The techs run across the river, which is about thirty feet across at this point and only knee deep. On the other side, they pull out their metal detectors and start sweeping the area as they continue to a place where the Black Hawk can land. Once they've checked the area for bombs, they run back, grab Donahue, and carry him across the river—not an easy feat, with the slippery rocks. They run to a wide-open spot and throw a red smoke marker down so the helo pilot can see them. They're still taking fire. The Black Hawk comes down in smoke and dust. And a minute later Corporal Max Donahue is lifted out of his hell and gone.

Later in the day doctors had to amputate one of Donahue's arms. His mother, Julie Schrock, sick with worry when she heard the news, took refuge in the fact that he was alive. If anyone could make a good life with three limbs missing, it would be her son. "He'd be joking around in no time, flirting with the nurses. He'd be an inspiration for anyone else who had to go through this."

But at 4:30 A.M. on August 6, 2010—two days after the explosion—she got the call from a military hospital in Landstuhl, Germany. Her son was brain dead. "Words can't describe the excruciating pain of that message," she says. "If only I could have just been there to hold him so he wouldn't have been alone." He wanted to be an organ donor, so Schrock was told they had to keep him alive another day until they could operate. That's why his official death date is listed as August 7.

The next day she got a package in the mail. It was from Max. A DVD, with photos and video snippets from Afghanistan. His family got out the laptop and watched it on the kitchen table until the last frame. It was a photo of him in full combat gear, just him and his rifle in the desert. Across it, these words: "See you soon—I miss you guys."

In death, as in life, Donahue was there for others. His death saved three lives in Europe. His liver helped a thirty-four-year-old man in liver failure. His right kidney went to a sixty-seven-year-old man who had waited for a kidney transplant for more than ten years. And a fourteen-year-old boy's life would change forever because of Donahue's left kidney.

His casket rolled slowly off the plane in Denver. Six marines dressed in their blues saluted in perfect unison. Schrock caught sight of her son's dog tags on the casket handle. They were undamaged, yet her son, inside his final resting place, was broken beyond repair. The thought made her nauseated and angry but mostly just numb.

At the packed funeral on August 13, his father said this:

"I loved the way you always stood up for the little guy or were willing to help someone in need. You hated bullies. And it didn't matter how big they were, either. They knew they had their hands full with Max Donahue. When you were growing up, all the little kids liked to hang with you because they felt they were safe. They knew you wouldn't let anything or anyone hurt them. You were their hero.

". . . I'm going to miss you, your laugh, your passion and compassion, and your love for life. You literally lived it to the 'max.' We all love you. And we're all so very proud of you. And every American that values their freedom should be proud of you, too, for the way you so bravely served your country. I know at times as a father I've let you down, but as a son you have never failed me. You're my hero. God bless you, Max."

CYCLE OF LIFE

Any soldier, sailor, airman, or marine who has ever served during wartime knows that with serving come loss, triumphs, partings, tragedies, and unbreakable bonds. But for dogs and handlers, it's all doubled, in a way, because there are two of you. You're a team within a team within a team, and you have your own dramas, your mutual losses and joys.

And while you're stronger because of each other, you're also each more vulnerable. Everything one of you does affects the other. If one of you gets hurt, the other is at a loss. You have to stop working. Without your other half, you can't function, and in fact, you are not allowed to keep working on your own. If it's bad enough, you mourn, and eventually you find a new teammate and go through the months of bonding and training and certifying that lead to life with a new other half. And you begin again.

But even without a loss of life or limb, bonds and partnerships are routinely forged and broken in the military dog world. Perhaps your dog needs to deploy before you can, so he goes off with a new handler. Or if you get shipped to a new base, in most cases your dog will not travel with you.

And so it is, comings and goings, beginnings and endings—a never-ending cycle of life and death is enacted all around you, both in your own microcosm of soldier dog and handler and in the universe of war that's your backdrop.

And when you think about all that this means, you see more clearly than ever that a soldier dog is so much more than just a piece of equipment. And you wonder: If these dogs also risk losing life and limb in combat, how should they be treated when they can no longer serve their country? Should treatment reflect their status as equipment, or as brother species-in-arms?

These questions lead to many others, some of which are tuned to cultural debates. Is man's best friend entitled to rights or just compassionate regard? What's fair treatment of these dogs? What's the right thing to do?

On their long nights of patrolling near the Panama Canal in the mid-1990s, Army Sergeant John Engstrom and Max P333 forged an indelible friendship in the midst of the dense jungle. When you walk together six miles every night in a foreign environment, the bond comes easily, as it tends to with expats. Engstrom and the long-haired shepherd would talk about politics and life while on alert for trouble. It was a one-way conversation, really, but that didn't matter to Engstrom. Max listened, looking intently at Engstrom when he came to emphatic points.

Max kept Engstrom's mind from the jungle laden with large spiders. In an elephant versus mouse scenario, the robust 195-pound man hated the creatures, and they were everywhere. During one patrol where Engstrom had to crawl on his belly alongside the canal looking for someone Max had alerted to, Engstrom ended up covered with hundreds of ticks—spiders' bloodthirsty cousins. They embedded quickly, and by the time the hospital started taking them out hours later, many were round and soft with Engstrom's blood. On their long patrols, Max couldn't keep the arachnids away physically, but the dog's presence kept them from overtaking Engstrom's imagination.

Max was an aggressive partner when he needed to be—a "real dog" in handler parlance. He bit the bad guys hard and with confidence. But with Engstrom's wife, the dog turned to mush. Max would start out dignified and well mannered, but within thirty seconds of her kindly attentions, "he'd wag so hard his ass shook, his ears would go back all happy and goofy." Max had almost nonstop ear infections, despite the best treatment, and she'd rub his ears just the right way, and the lethal weapon would purr.

Engstrom had to say good-bye to his partner in early 1995. They had been reassigned to others. Later that year, Engstrom left Panama because U.S. presence was drawing down. But he didn't forget that dog.

Back in the U.S., Engstrom ended up at Lackland Air Force Base, instructing green handlers from all services in the art of working with military dogs. As part of the job, he'd routinely take them on tours of the base. In June 1997, he was showing a small group the dog hospital. He saw that there was something going on in the necropsy lab.

A military dog necropsy isn't the relatively tame affair you see on *NCIS*. A series of knives, one bigger than the other, hang on a magnetic strip on the wall, as at a butcher shop. Dozens of smaller, shiny cutting-and-grabbing instruments lie on a tray off the foot of the necropsy table: hemostats, tweezers, clamps, rib cutters, a steel mallet. Sinks and vats catch fluids and parts. It is a scientific business. Since there is no chance of an open-casket funeral, dogs are cut and opened with everything hanging out in ways you don't want to imagine. Sometimes just the head is recognizable. Sometimes not.

Engstrom opened the door to the necropsy lab and brought his students in. They approached the table on which the splayed mess that was once someone's comrade was ready for disposal. And then Engstrom saw it. The head, the odd Cyrillic tattoo from his original breeder, and the other tattooed ear he knew so well from all those ear infection solutions he'd massaged in.

It was Max.

Engstrom doesn't remember much after that. Just shock, followed by a sick, empty feeling. A hole in his own gut. "Man, they cut him apart." He went home after that. Or maybe he didn't. He can't remember. The nightmare fogged the day. You don't want to see a friend like that, he explains. You should never see a friend like that. For months it was hard to shake the image, the sickening shock. He never tried to find out why Max had been euthanized at age eight. He thinks the dog had hip issues, but he just couldn't bring himself to ask.

★ ★ ★ 48 ★ ★ ★

"THE WORST KIND OF

ANIMAL ABUSE"

Necropsies are performed on every military working dog who dies in service. The extent of an ailment isn't always apparent on the outside. These dogs have so much heart and drive that it masks signs of just how bad things are on the inside. And then you cut them open on the necropsy slab, and you're stunned that a dog with that kind of cancer or other great physical problem could still carry on.

Before the law changed in 2000, when federal legislation dubbed "the Robby law" passed, bite-trained dogs who were no longer able to work were considered unadoptable. The liability was deemed too much. They were sometimes transferred to other law-enforcement agencies, but more often they were euthanized.

Many people, even those steeped in the military working dog world, are under the impression that before 2000, the Department of Defense euthanized *all* dogs who were unable to be working dogs, if they were not transferred to law enforcement. It turns out this is not true. I'm told that non-attack-trained dogs were usually adopted out. Lackland provided me with a spreadsheet of dogs adopted by individuals from 1983 through 1999. There are 192 dogs on the list. Their ranks include a number of beagles and Labrador retrievers, and even a cairn terrier. But the majority of the dogs on the list are Belgian Malinois or German shepherds. It can be assumed that most of these dogs were purchased by the Department of Defense and then didn't make it through training. They may have been lovers, not fighters. More puzzling to me are the few dogs who have "Patrol" or "Patrol/Explosive" listed as their occupation. Maybe these dogs were so old and decrepit that they were harmless. Perhaps they even went to their handlers, who knew how to deal with them. Fewer than two hundred dogs in seventeen years is nothing compared with today's thriving adoption program, but it is a worthy footnote in the history of military working dog adoption.

The routine euthanization of most dogs outraged people like former Marine Captain William Putney, who had commanded a war-dog platoon in World War II and watched dogs giving their lives for their country for years during the war.

"To use animals for our own use and then destroy them arbitrarily when they can no longer be of use to us is the worst kind of animal abuse," he would write in a letter that was read to Congress in support of the Robby law.

He never got over the bravery and loyalty he saw in these dogs. And decades later, he was still struck by incredible feats he saw and the bonds he witnessed.

In 1944, Putney was leading a patrol to find some entrenched Japanese during the invasion of Guam. Suddenly there was gunfire, and a bullet slammed into a Doberman named Cappy and tore a hole in his chest. The dog was walking just in front of Putney, and the bullet would have been his if not for Cappy. The dog's handler was overcome. He "picked the body up and held it in his arms with blood all over his face—he was crying, just rocking back and forth. . . . He'd lost his buddy," Putney told *The Washington Post* in 2000.

Putney, who became chief veterinarian of the Marine Corps after the war, did not buy the idea that these dogs were a liability—something the Department of Defense would put forth for the next fifty years. "It is not true that once a dog has had attack training, it can never be released safely into the civilian population," he wrote in his letter.

He knew from experience that the majority of these dogs could be safely re-homed: The 550 marine war dogs serving at the end of World War II had all been trained to attack, but he says only four were put down because they could not be "detrained" well enough for civilian life. The rest of the dogs were adopted out. He says that to his knowledge, none of those dogs ever attacked or hurt anyone. This was done throughout the military with similar success.

But that lesson was lost in the Vietnam era. Some thirty-eight hundred dogs deployed there and are credited with saving many thousands of lives while protecting troops, leading jungle patrols, and detecting ambushes and mines. But the military deemed the dogs too dangerous to return home. Indeed, many of the sentry dogs had been trained to be so vicious that even their handlers had a hard time controlling them.

But sentry dogs were just one type of dog in the war. There were others, including scouts and trackers. Still, only about two hundred dogs would ever return home. Besides the behavioral issues, there was worry that even the less violent dogs would carry disease from Southeast Asia—something that could have been circumvented by a quarantine once they were home.

The majority of dogs were left behind or euthanized.

My friend Sylvana Stratton's father was one of the few to be able to adopt one of these dogs. He had befriended a scout dog's handler while in Vietnam. Her father, Harold Thomason, was then a sergeant. He had a way with animals and was one of only a couple of people the German shepherd, King, would accept.

One day, King's handler went out on a covert mission without King. He stepped on a land mine and was paralyzed from the waist down. He immediately flew Stateside for treatment, recuperation, and medical retirement.

Thomason was the only person who could handle King, so he would visit the kennel daily and walk him and feed him. Eventually he was authorized to take the dog as his own.

Thomason applied for an exception to bring King home when his assignment was up. He had to go through miles of red tape to get the approval. He knew that if King didn't come home with him, the dog was never coming home. Thomason finally got approval and arranged for a commercial transport for the dog to come back to the States. It cost about $700—a big chunk of change in the early 1970s.

King lived with Thomason and his family for a couple of years and had no problems with family members. But Stratton says it was a struggle to have to keep the dog separated from guests—especially when she and her brother always had friends coming and going.

"I forgot one day," Stratton says, "and the dog lunged at my date, who luckily put his arm up and was bitten in the arm and not the throat, which is where he was heading." The dog had to go.

Her father decided to track down the paralyzed handler, who lived alone, with no family nearby. The man was ecstatic to have King back again. King remained his great companion until the dog died several years later. There were no more incidents of violence.

In a way, it was understandable that the Defense Department balked at allowing dogs to have a better fate. After all, even King, a rare dog allowed to return from Vietnam, was not entirely trust-worthy. But dogs are no longer trained as sentries, or even as some scout dogs had been. Patrol dogs are far more controllable, and many can take care of business one minute and come back and be everyone's best pal the next. In 2000, it was time for this antiquated policy to be brought into the new millennium.

Putney had watched the devastation so many Vietnam-era handlers went through when forced to leave their canine comrades behind. To this day, many handlers cannot talk about their dogs; it's just too painful. He would do whatever it took to prevent this from happen-ing again. In 2000 he got his chance.

Representative Roscoe G. Bartlett (R-MD) had taken note of an article in *Stars and Stripes* that pointed out what happens to dogs at the end of their careers. The article had mentioned a dog named Robby W005, a dual-purpose Belgian Malinois who was suffering from bad arthritis, elbow dysplasia, and a painful growth on his spine. He was no longer able to work—no longer even able to be considered as a training aide (a desk job, as it were) at Lackland. His handler wanted to adopt him, but the rules prevented that.

Bartlett vowed to do something. In a move widely supported by animal agencies and the public, he introduced HR 5314 (which would become the Robby law), which allowed adoption of any military dog deemed adoptable by the Department of Defense. New owners were to bear the liability. Putney was one of many who came out in favor of the bill. He wrote:

> *Our service dogs must be honored and treated as heroes because that is what they are. And they must be allowed to retire to loving homes, as any soldier is. They have served us with honor and distinction, and have saved countless American sons and daughters from injury and death. They have risked their own death and injury for no more than the love and affection of their handlers.*
>
> *They would never, ever have left us behind, and they would never give up on us because we were too old or infirm to do our jobs anymore. If they can offer us this sort of service and devotion, how can we do less for them? We owe them.*

With support like this, Bartlett was able to ramrod the bill through Congress. The vote was unanimous. Bill Clinton signed the bill into law two months after Bartlett had introduced it.

The law would save thousands of soldier dogs in the future, including at least one who shared its name. . . .

★ ★ ★ 49 ★ ★ ★

A NICE RETIREMENT

When former Air Force Staff Sergeant James Bailey takes walks in his quiet Richmond, Virginia, neighborhood with his Belgian Malinois, Robby D131, people take note. "Is that the dog that got Osama bin Laden?" they want to know. Robby is something of a celebrity these days since that other Malinois, Cairo, played his secret role in helping the Navy SEALs take down Bin Laden.

Robby was Bailey's first military working dog and already a veteran when they met. He'd done two deployments to Iraq and one to Kuwait. The war vet, age eight, and his handler, twenty-one, got on like old friends from the start. Soldier dogs don't seem to harden, even after several tours and different handlers.

Robby and his green handler deployed for six months in November 2008 in Camp Taji, Iraq. Robby was a patient teacher. "For the first few weeks he took the lead and pretty much showed me how things worked. He made me a better handler by 'understanding' that I was new to things, and it almost seemed as if he took his time in the beginning because he knew that. He searched much more slowly in the beginning compared to at the end of his working career, when we were flying through our training problems without missing a beat."

The old dog provided support beyond the technical. "He's always had my back. He was always there to make sure I was OK, whether he needed to help protect me, or when I was a little down and he'd come over and put his head in my lap. He could read my body language, he could read my emotions, like no one else could."

After numerous missions outside the wire, the team returned to Seymour Johnson Air Force Base, North Carolina, and settled in for a couple of years.

But when Bailey's turn for deployment came up again in 2010, he couldn't take Robby. The dog's back had gone bad in the interim. He had been diagnosed with lumbosacral disease, a compression of nerve roots in the area where a dog's spine meets his hips. It's not uncommon in larger dogs. In bad cases, nerve impairment can lead to weakness in rear limbs and even incontinence. Robby's case was relatively mild, and the pain could be controlled by medication. But he was not fit for another deployment.

Bailey was relieved in a way—at least the old man would be safe—and went off to an undisclosed location with a four-year-old German shepherd named Ajax L523. They bonded, as soldiers do, "but nothing like Robby and me."

When Bailey returned six months later, Robby, who had been living in the base's kennel, had not forgotten his friend.

"I walked around the corner of the kennel and he dropped his ears back and was wagging his tail like crazy. It was kind of cool because he still knew exactly who I was."

Robby, now eleven and white of muzzle, has a new assignment: He has retired and will spend his remaining time with Bailey, who left the air force at the same time he adopted Robby. "I just wanted to get him out of the kennel and get him home so he could have a good couple of years before the end."

They live together in a house with a fenced backyard and all the toys a dog could want. "It is absolutely wonderful having him at home. I like to call him my shadow. If I go to a different room, so does Robby. He follows me all over and will just lay and watch me do chores or lay on the patio while I cut the grass."

Robby sleeps on a large tea-green orthopedic dog bed (a big improvement over the concrete floors of kennels he slept on for years) next to Bailey's other dog, a sixty-five-pound shelter mutt named Gunner. Gunner is Robby's first real dog friend, since working dogs are generally not allowed to fraternize with other dogs in the service.

"It's a pretty awesome feeling to give Robby a safe, comfortable home. He kept me safe while we were in Iraq and protected so many people. It's great to be able to give back to him and try to repay the lifelong sacrifice he has given to me, his other handlers, and the country."

But what about the day when Robby is in too much pain to go on, the day Bailey has to make the decision no pet owner wants to face? Bailey pauses and takes a breath. "It won't be easy, but I'll know it's my turn to help him and I'll be there for him," he says. On his walls hang framed pictures of the two of them. After Robby goes, Bailey plans to make a tribute wall or a shadow box to memorialize him. "That way I can always show him off and give him the respect he deserves, even after he's gone."

And one more thing. He hesitates. It may sound kind of weird, he forewarns. "I'd like to think that one day we will be able to play fetch again on the other side."

50

THE ADOPTION CRAZE

In early 2011, John Engstrom, the former handler who had the shock of finding his old dog in the necropsy room, got a new job at Lackland. It's a position he wishes existed when Max was still around. Engstrom, now a civilian, is the adoption coordinator for the military working dog adoption program. He has come full circle, in a way, from that terrible day in 1997.

When he started the job in March 2011, there was already a long list of people who wanted to adopt military working dogs. Engstrom had his work cut out for him. But that was child's play compared to what would happen less than two months later, when the world learned a military dog took part in taking out the world's most wanted terrorist. All hell broke loose. "The phone has been ringing off the hook since May 1," he told me months later. "Everyone and his brother and sister and aunt wants one of these dogs now."

Many people who call here want to adopt Cairo. It seems a lot of people don't even realize there *are* other military working dogs, Engstrom says.

Engstrom breaks the news about Cairo (that he's not here, and he's certainly not up for adoption), and then goes on to inform callers that some available for adoption are dog school washouts. These dogs might be gun-shy or slow to learn important skills. They're good dogs with flaws that make them less-than-ideal military dogs. Many dogs on the adoption roster are training aids who may or may not have served overseas before becoming a little old or stiff for the work. Few dogs up for adoption to the public have recently deployed; one or more of the handlers of those dogs will usually step up to claim the dog before the dog is even retired.

Something Engstrom tries to remember to tell callers is that while the available dogs may be highly trained and very well bred, many are not house-trained. Think about it. The dogs live in kennels, where they do their business whenever and wherever. A few have stayed in hotels, so they probably have been trained. Those who stay in tents on deployment may have gotten the general idea that you saunter outside when nature calls. But most of these dogs have never set foot in a house.

Of all the skills a military dog needs to know, the locale in which to do his business is not among them. Jake may not know how to sniff out IEDs, and he's no attack dog, but I'll say this for him: He doesn't use our floor as a toilet. Fortunately the military dogs are fast studies, and usually it just takes a couple of times until they learn the ropes.

While Engstrom is in charge of adoptions through Lackland, other bases around the United States and abroad adopt out dogs, as well. Unless a dog is already at Lackland as a dog school student or training aid, or is there to be checked out medically at Lackland's veterinary hospital, the dog will be adopted straight from his home base.

Engstrom does his best to encourage people to fill out the applications or, if they're far away, to contact local military dog kennels to see about "dispo'd" dogs in need of adoption. Plenty do. "They want to help these great American heroes," he says.

The average wait for a member of the public (you and me, as opposed to handlers or law-enforcement agencies) to adopt a dog at Lackland is about eighteen months, but that may fade as the Bin Laden story fades into the past. Handlers and law enforcement get top priority, depending on the dog and the situation. If a dog's handler wants to adopt his old dog, she'll usually take precedence. There's a waiting list of about sixty law-enforcement agencies hoping to get their hands on a good dog with a strong drive for a reward. They're not looking for war heroes. And about forty to fifty new applications from the public come in each month. Only five to ten dogs get eliminated from the training program during the same time frame. That makes for a backlog of willing homes.

Whether or not the would-be adopters qualify is another matter altogether.

Engstrom has heard it all from potential adopters. I promised him I would not give away key words or phrases that make him automatically suspect a home is not suitable for adoption. The dogs are to be pets, nothing more, certainly nothing less. I won't go beyond that, because he needs to do the screening his own way, and I don't want anyone getting clues and circumventing his process.

He doesn't hesitate to talk in general terms, however, about the breadth of people who want to invite a military working dog into their lives. On one end are the people who want a fearsome dog and are probably up to no good. On the other are the people who write pages and pages of flowery prose about how they are psychically in tune with a dog who is sending them messages that they were always meant to be together, that no other match must be made, and who cares if they're eighteen months down the waiting list— their intuition is never wrong and they must have that dog (whoever he or she is) now.

The barking frenzy in the adoption kennels is at a fever pitch, but I can still hear Engstrom. His voice sometimes hits the excited praise notes of trainers and handlers, and at other times it's quiet and more reverential and serious. It depends on the dog we're passing.

"What's up there, handsome stranger?! Nigel! *Niiigellllll!* Isn't he a dark handsome wonder?!"

"There's Bono. You are an *excellent* dog. He's got degenerative arthritis in his hips. Poor guy."

"Asta! Your new parents are coming to get you today! Isn't she a beautiful color?"

"This is Jerry. Jerry is really cool. He's always down for fun."

"Pepper! You're going to be in the San Antonio police department! Way to go!!"

We stop at Buck's kennel. He's the one with canine post-traumatic stress disorder. "Hang in there, buddy. Tomorrow you're going home with a couple who loves you a lot."

Buck's neighbor is Rony. He is a beautiful German shepherd— everything a shepherd should be, from his regal stature to his alert demeanor. I instantly like this dog. He's not barking, but he's not curled up. He's just kingly. I get his tattoo number, R262. He's young, then, since this is an R year for tattoos. He may be two or three. He probably failed dog school. I learn that Rony has a paralyzing fear of thunderstorms. He literally bites the cage sides of his kennel and pulls his way up the kennel wall, nearly hanging from the ceiling, during storms. In San Francisco we get thunder maybe once a year. Rony wouldn't be so tormented. I could see this dog in my house, passing the storm-free days away snoozing next to Jake. But I was nowhere in the running. I hadn't even filled out an application yet.

I was worried about this fellow, but everyone told me there are few storms in San Antonio that time of year—especially with the wicked drought that was going on. I felt better knowing that Rony wouldn't have to deal with storms while living in his kennel. At least next time one hit, he'd likely be in the comfort of someone's home.

That night, as I drove to the airport, I was caught in a storm so torrential I had to pull off the side of the road with all the other traffic. The thunder was so strong I could feel it in my chest. I worried about Rony. I wished I'd filled out an adoption form eighteen months ago.

★

But would Rony have been a good match for our household? Would Rony have eaten Jake, lunged at family and friends? I didn't bother finding out, because what if he was a teddy bear? I'd want to take him home even more than I already did, and that just wasn't happening.

By the time the dogs are put up for adoption, they've been

through behavioral testing. And any dog who was ever trained in patrol work will have gone through something called a bite muzzle test. This involves testing how much attack a dog has left in him. It's a somewhat complex process that shows what a dog will or won't do under various conditions. Dogs who are not at Lackland are videotaped doing the test. The video is sent to Lackland, where, together with reading about a dog's history, behavior experts can use it to evaluate how safe the dog might be for adoption.

Even if a dog isn't perfect, he can still be adopted. Engstrom just has to be more selective about homes. Many bite-trained military working dogs are dog-aggressive even when they retire. It's partly their socialization (or lack thereof; the dogs don't get to interact much with one another) and partly the stock they come from and perhaps the fact that these dogs are not neutered. Whatever the case, Engstrom obviously won't adopt a dog-aggressive dog to a home with another dog. If dogs are a little edgy, they won't get to be in homes with children. There are plenty of couples and single people living in remote areas who would be more than happy to take these dogs. But if the dog-aggression is bad enough, the dog is euthanized.

This dog-aggression is something that many in the military working dog world would like to see change. Some are trying to get dogs more acclimated to each other by letting them have play time together, off leash, in a fenced area. They have to be monitored carefully, but it often works well. "They have to get used to each other. It's not safe to have so much aggression toward other dogs. The dogs are not supposed to be fighting other dogs," Arod told me.

Many health issues won't preclude adoption unless it would be cruel for the dog to be kept alive only to suffer. A dog with a terminal illness but who is pain free and seems to have a lot of time left could be considered for adoption. There's no shortage of people who would adopt a dog to give him comfort and love in his last months.

Before the Robby law, Engstrom says, "it was extremely sad. We kept dogs working that had no business working, because there was no alternative. You would see dogs that literally had almost complete organ failure. We weren't willing to give up these dogs to so easily die."

I met a dog at Travis Air Force Base who was deploying the next day. He was twelve years old. He already had seven deployments under his belt. I was stunned that such an old dog would still be deploying. But the handlers told me that deploying was what was saving him from death: While this dog was a pussycat with his most recent handler, who had been with him for a few months, if he didn't know you, watch out. He was extremely aggressive.

The handlers there are amazed that he is going so strong at twelve. They have a theory. They think he knows that if he doesn't keep working, he's done for. It's the only explanation the handlers I interviewed could come up with. "He must know it, somehow."

The average age of retirement is now about 8.3 years. Some people would like to see dogs retired before they start having too many physical ailments, so they can get a little pain-free enjoyment out of civilian life. But with Department of Defense budgets in distress, it's unlikely that highly functional dogs will be let out early just to enjoy some couch time before arthritis sets in.

In 2010, the Department of Defense adopted out 304 dogs and transferred 34 to law enforcement. Eight dispo'd dogs who were healthy enough to be adopted were put down because they were deemed too dangerous for adoption. Twelve temperamentally adoptable dogs had to be euthanized because of serious health issues that would have caused intractable pain.

Some say the numbers of adoptions would increase if the government would bring dogs who are retired while overseas back home. We're not talking about dogs being abandoned on the streets of Kabul, as some who have heard about this issue seem to think. This is mostly about dogs who are left at permanent U.S. bases in places like Germany when they're deemed unable to work. As it is, an adoptable dog stays at the base until adopted. If people in the United States want to adopt the dog, they have to pay for the dog to return home.

The official argument is this: Dogs, as hard as it may be to swallow, are still considered equipment. When standard equipment (without a cold nose and a tail) is pulled out of operation, it's not sent back to where it came from. So if a dog is retired overseas, you don't send him back to the States, even if that's where he got his initial training. And military budgets have been crippled with the economic downturn. The government doesn't want to be paying for dogs to come back to the States if private individuals will foot the bill.

Debbie Kandoll, founder of the group Military Working Dog Adoptions, calls this hogwash. "Uncle Sam transported those military working dog heroes over to permanent bases abroad. Uncle Sam has a responsibility to get the dog back to the continental U.S.," she says. "There is no reason that half-empty U.S. military aircraft cannot transport these dogs back to CONUS [the continental United States]. At that point the adopter can pay for transport to the dog's new residence."

She says many people have adopted dogs from overseas sight

unseen. They get information from the kennel master and the dog's handler, and if they like the dog, they figure out how to make it work. (On her Web site she gives tips for situations like this and provides contact information for U.S. military dog kennels Stateside and around the world.) It takes time and money to do this. I've heard figures ranging from $400 to $2,000 for transport, depending on location, time of year, and size of dog.

In order for retiring dogs to be flown back home on the government's bill, these dogs would need to be reclassified as MWD veterans instead of excess equipment, Kandoll says. Her group and a few others are pushing for an amendment to the Robby law that would make this possible. "We can't let an ocean stand in the way of getting these deserving dogs wonderful homes," she says.

51

A VERY GOOD LIFE

I t's not just people who adopt from overseas locations who put a Herculean effort into adopting a military working dog. While I was at Lackland, I met a couple who drove 1,047 miles, from rural Illinois, to pick up their dog. That the pickup happened to coincide with a wedding a few hours away was pure luck. "We'd have come down for her no matter what," says Jerry Self, president of an engineering firm in Illinois.

Self heard about military dogs in December 2009, when a friend sent him a link to a video about the fact that the dogs need good homes when they retire. Shortly after, he put in his paperwork. In early 2011, Engstrom called to talk to him, to get to know more about his situation, and to give him the news that it wouldn't be long now.

Self and his wife, Karen, had been in San Antonio for two days when I met them at Engstrom's desk at Lackland. They were there to pick up Asta—the beautiful light fawn-colored Malinois I'd seen earlier in the kennel. They'd met her a couple of days earlier as they were looking for a good match. Self thought he wanted an old war vet German shepherd, but he and his wife saw Asta and knew she was the one. "There was something about the way she looked at us," he told me.

Asta was only two years old. She was as green as they come. She had not received much military training, because she had gotten injured and had fractured a vertebra near the end of her spine. She had undergone surgery, but she was compromised, and the vets didn't think it would be wise to put her into the program.

I waited to watch the Selfs and Asta meet in the adoption room and for them to walk off to their car with their new dog. But it turned out that Asta needed a couple more official clearances before they could bring her home. So they'd stay in San Antonio one more night. They were disappointed but took it in stride. "We waited this long, what's another day or two?" Self said.

"She's going to have a good life with us."

We kept in touch. Asta rode the 1,047 miles home to Casey, Illinois, like a trouper, never a peep, Jerry Self wrote me. They stopped for breaks pretty often, and when they stayed at hotels along the way, Asta slept in her crate. There were no accidents, there was no barking.

Back at home, Asta was gentle with the Selfs' grandchildren, and with their Chihuahua, who is grouchy about Asta being there. The Selfs don't think Asta would have been a good patrol dog because "there's not a mean bone in her body. She loves affection, and she gets quite a lot."

Asta has a thing for Frisbees. She owns about a dozen, and while she likes to chase after them, she prefers to fold them taco style and trot around with them. When Jerry Self goes to throw them, they wobble badly because of all the teeth marks. And she slobbers on everything. And she is high energy. "She gallops around like a horse most of the time. . . . She is young and rambunctious and likes to jump up on the couch and office furniture, and knocks everything down," Jerry says.

In fact, the Selfs find that at this stage, life is a bit more tame when Asta is enjoying time in a special 110- by 80-foot fenced-in area they built around their house for her. It has big trees and grass in it. Squirrels scamper up and down the trees, and the family's three cats like to bask in the sunshine and watch the latest addition to the household. She doesn't pay them much mind, though. She's just enjoying her newfound life in this lush, green, bucolic land—a long, long way from the war zone where she could well be right now had she not been injured.

Which brings me back to Jake. If not for his own accident—an accident of birth—*could* he have been a military working dog? Would he have withstood the rigors of training, of Yuma, of deployment? Would he have learned to fiercely guard a Kong, to want it so badly he would do anything for it?

He has the spirit, the loyalty, the can-do attitude. He has patience, a great nose, no crippling fears. But does he have the drive? Would he be willing to do anything for a reward? Since

I can take a Kong or tennis ball out of his mouth and have him shrug it off with a smile, his drive for that kind of reward is not strong enough.

But what about food? He lives for food. (He is a Lab, say no more.) I think he could be one of those dogs for whom food is the reward that would lift him to great heights. But the dog program tends to frown on food rewards, as do most trainers these days, and he'd need so many treats he'd probably get so obese, he'd be dispo'd anyway.

The bottom line, though, really goes beyond whether or not he could have been a contender. As much as I have tremendous, undying admiration for military working dogs and their handlers—even more than when I began this journey—and as much fun as it is to fantasize that Jake could have the right stuff to be a soldier dog, I would not want him to actually do the job. I can't imagine anyone these days really wanting his or her dog to go to war, be in harm's way. Even most handlers would like their dogs to be with them somewhere other than military kennels, or FOBs, or outside the wire.

That's why so many end up adopting. "I wanted him to know what it was like to be a regular dog in a regular house, before he crossed the bridge," I was told in various ways many times. It's something many of us take for granted, but imagine being the dog who suddenly finds herself away from war, away from the blasts of artillery, IEDs, the adrenaline, the heat, the loud concrete kennels. Imagine living in a comfortable home, with a soft bed, and a loving family. It must be like a dream.

There's one situation where it would be handy if Jake were a military working dog, though—especially now that he's getting a bit on in years: whenever he needs medical care. The medical care these dogs receive would be prohibitively expensive for most of us and is first-rate. It makes my health insurance look rather primitive.

★ ★ ★ 52 ★ ★ ★

THE BEST MEDICAL CARE
MONEY CAN BUY

Ttitan N319 slowly slides into the CT scanner. He's on his
back, paws in the air. As he enters the tube, a red laser shines
on him, creating interesting arcs and lines on his paws and then on
his rear end and, finally, his tail, until he's all the way in. A technician is beside him, making sure all is well. Outside the room, other
CT pros, including two veterinary radiologists, look on, noting the
dog's image on a large computer screen in front of them. He's a
Malinois, but in black-and-white, with the perspective of this particular view from the scanner, he looks rather like a lizard.

This is a high-end CT scanner he's in, but he'll never know it,
because he's out cold. (He would not know it anyway, I suppose.)
Nearly everything at the Daniel E. Holland Military Working
Dog Hospital at Lackland Air Force Base is state-of-the-art.
Opened in 2008 and named after an army veterinarian who was
killed in Iraq, the $13 million hospital is a unique referral center
providing top-notch veterinary care for pretty much every issue a
soldier dog could face. If they can't take care of it here—for instance,
if a dog needs an MRI, something the MWD hospital lacks—a dog

can be taken to the human medical center at Lackland. MRIs are scheduled during non-human-patient hours.

When the veterinary hospital bought the CT scanner being occupied by Ttitan, it was better than the one at the human medical center. Ttitan is being examined for a previous injury. He's looking good so far. My guide, Kelly Mann, a veterinary radiologist and director of the hospital, ushers us on.

Down the hall and through a few large, superclean exam and treatment rooms we come to a boxful of light blue shoe covers. Mann asks me to put on a pair, and he does the same. We then enter a small, darkened room and come to a large window that looks into a large, state-of-the-art surgical suite. It's one of two at the hospital. A team of two veterinarians (one visiting from Korea) and two vet techs surrounds the patient. You cannot see there's a dog under all that surgical draping, and you'd swear it must be a person until you see a tiny hint of a paw. This dog has a bad carpus (basically, a dog's wrist) injury, and today is getting a procedure called arthrodesis to fix the carpus in place. It should greatly reduce the pain he's been having.

After his surgery, he'll be taken to the recovery area, which has heated floors. During his weeks of recovery, he'll eventually end up in what they call the "gee whiz room." This is the part of the physical therapy department that has underwater treadmills designed just for dogs. The body weight of a dog on one of these treadmills is greatly reduced, making weight-bearing exercise more bearable. It's one of the first steps in exercise rehab.

It's clear that soldier dogs who come to this hospital are in very good hands. Since it's a referral hospital, the facility gets military dogs from everywhere. Veterinary care at most bases with kennels is usually very good, but the vets know when something is beyond them or their facility, and they don't hesitate to send dogs here. (The hospital also treats TSA and Border Patrol dogs.)

You might think, "Well sure, they're giving this equipment good treatment because they have to keep the dog ready to protect lives, just like you'd service a military plane or even a rifle." And there may be some truth to that. The idea is to keep these dogs healthy and able to work. But many of the patients here will never be going back to work. Their careers are ending because of medical issues. It's heartening to see that the Department of Defense doesn't turn its back on them just because they're no longer of use.

"We fix them at the end of their career, even if we adopt them out. It's the right thing to do," says Mann.

The hospital's necropsy room is not far off the lobby of the hospital. It is very spacious, with two tables and all the accoutrements needed for the deep level of necropsy done here. This is not where Engstrom found what was left of Max; that was in the old hospital. But it's a stark reminder that even with all the best treatment, soldier dogs die. And if you're a soldier dog, it is pretty much guaranteed you'll get a necropsy.

This isn't just to see what went wrong inside a dog; the knowledge gained from these procedures can help other dogs. A dog's tissues are sent to the Joint Pathology Center, where the samples are prepared for histopathology and read out by board-certified veterinary pathologists. Eventually, all of those results and the complete medical records are mailed to the MWD medical records repository. The end-of-life data are reviewed retrospectively by the staff epidemiologist, to keep veterinarians informed of the most common diseases being seen in the soldier dog population. This helps them refine the topics that are taught to Veterinary Corps officers and animal care specialists who are taking basic and advanced courses there, and the information helps the operational units learn of common issues to watch for in the working dog population.

So there's a lot of potential good that comes from necropsies, but the notion of what a dog looks like—what poor Engstrom saw—after one of these makes me shudder. I would not want Jake to go through this. Most handlers want to be with their dog for euthanasia but won't stick around for the necropsy because it's just too much.

When a soldier dog dies, if the dog is lucky enough to have a handler (as opposed to dogs who are training aids), the dog will not be forgotten. Handlers can get the cremated remains of what's not sent off to pathologists. Depending on the base where the necropsy occurred, the handler may get the ashes back in a beautifully engraved wood box. Some bases have memorial walls where the boxes are placed next to photos of the dog. Others have small cemeteries devoted to their military working dogs.

Amanda Ingraham buried Rex's ashes at Fort Myer before she left for Germany with Cinte. She and her father worked together to make a cross with Rex's name deeply engraved in it. She didn't have time for a traditional dog memorial, but she will when she returns.

And she's not looking forward to trying to read the poem that handlers traditionally read during these ceremonies. She'll probably have someone else do it, because she can't get through the last few lines.

The poem, "Guardians of the Night," speaks of the bond military dogs (or police dogs, depending on the version you read) have with their handlers, from a dog's point of view. In the end, the poem talks about when their time has come to move on, and how for a time they were an unbeatable team, and then goes on to a couple of lines about what they'll do if they should ever meet again "on another field." This is where a lot of handlers break down. It's not great poetry. But if you picture your own dog, you're done for. (This poem is also read at handler course graduation ceremonies at Lackland, but it doesn't pack the emotional wallop it does at memorial services.)

There's another tradition at MWD memorial services. The dog's bowls are placed upside down, to symbolize that the dog won't need them anymore. The collar and leash are hung in remembrance of the dog. And if the memorial is at a kennel, the dog's kennel door is left open, indicating that the dog will not be returning home.

★ ★ ★ 53 ★ ★ ★

THIRTEEN MEDALS AND RIBBONS

Sergeant Mark Vierig, the marine we met earlier with his combat tracking dog, Lex, had worked with another dog a few years before. The dog was a dual-purpose Malinois, a big ninety-pounder named Duc B016. "He was an amazing dog," Vierig will tell you. Their bond ran deep. Duc (pronounced Duck) was always cool under fire, with a nose that sniffed out many a bomb in his day. He'd been to Afghanistan with Vierig, and to Iraq (twice), and even Thailand.

Vierig was able to adopt Duc in 2006, when Duc was ten or eleven years old. Vierig had left the marines after his four years of active duty (he was later called back in from inactive duty, which is where he met Lex) and was living with his wife, baby daughter, and four dogs in the mountains of Utah, next to the Weber River—a fly fisherman's paradise, and heaven on earth for the retired dog. Just the kind of place Duc deserved, Vierig told his friends.

On a summer day about a year after his grand new life started, Duc went outside and Vierig's wife saw him collapse. She yelled to Vierig, who ran out and found Duc unresponsive. He scooped the dog up and brought him inside the "Duc Room," a special room they had converted for Duc's comfort. Vierig sat down cross-legged on the floor, supporting Duc's head and upper body in his arms. He stroked his old face and neck, trying to figure out what was wrong. Suddenly Duc howled like a wolf, a plaintive cry Vierig had never heard before. Duc took one last breath and died in Vierig's arms.

Overcome by the sudden loss, and that primal howl, Vierig held his dog, telling him how much he loved him, how much Duc meant to him. Eventually he covered Duc with a brand-new 4-by-6-foot Marine Corps flag. He lay it over Duc's body. "He had done so much for me, I wanted to do right by him."

Within moments, four dogs Vierig was training for police and private companies entered the room. They were all energetic working dogs—a golden retriever, two Malinois, and a German shepherd. They'd revered Duc in life. They would run around and nip and chase and tackle one another, but they would leave him in peace. Now the dogs—every one of them—lay down quietly in a semicircle next to Duc's flag-draped body. They were not sleeping, but lying attentively, calmly. They stayed like this for twenty minutes. These independent-natured dogs never would lie next to each other—much less Duc—like this.

"They were paying respects to a dog who was deeply respected. That's not anthropomorphism," Vierig says. "If you'd seen it, you'd know."

Vierig wanted Duc's grave to be near the river, where fishermen walk by, so others would remember his friend, even if they had never met him. He wanted them to know that here lay a great dog. He dug a deep grave in a tree-filled area across the river and came back for Duc. Vierig wrapped Duc's body in the marine flag, picked up the ninety-pound dog, and hoisted him across the back of his shoulders. He walked him out his backyard and crossed the chest-deep water of the Weber, making sure to keep Duc dry. He lay Duc on the ground under a big tree with lots of shade.

Then he placed Duc in the grave, buried him, and covered the site with big round stones from the riverbed to help keep other animals from digging down. Earlier in the day he had attached to the tree Duc's old military kennel sign with his name on it. To this, he attached all of Duc's medals and ribbons. There were about thirteen, but since military working dogs don't officially rate ribbons and medals, they were actually all Vierig's, for anything he earned while Duc was his dog.

Vierig has since moved, but he still goes up to visit his dog and replaces ribbons when they wear out.

★ ★ ★ 54 ★ ★ ★

WHO NEEDS MEDALS OR STAMPS?

Duc got his ribbons the way many dogs do: unofficially, and because of someone's great admiration and respect. Dogs in the military are not officially awarded ribbons or medals from the Department of Defense. America's canine heroes can save all the lives in their squad and get injured in the process, but they will not receive true official recognition.

When you hear about dogs garnering awards and decorations, it's usually because someone higher up at a command knows how valuable these dogs are and wants to award their valor, their heroism, their steadfast dedication to their mission. And the dogs get the awards, but the awards don't have the blessing of the Department of Defense. One former army handler I spoke with says he has seen dogs get all kinds of honors, including Meritorious Service Medals and Army Commendation Medals. Some dogs have also received Purple Hearts and Silver Stars. The ceremonies look official. But these are simply "feel-good honors," says Ron Aiello, president of the national nonprofit organization the United States War Dogs Association.

For the last several years, Aiello and his group, which helps soldier dogs and their handlers, have been among a few organizations trying to get more official recognition of military working dogs. So far, the Department of Defense hasn't budged.

Aiello's group has been told medals and awards are only for human troops, not animals. Aiello is sensitive to the fact that giving a dog the same award as a person might be a touchy subject for some. So he proposed a special service medal just for dogs. That didn't work, either. Finally, "because the DOD had no interest in awarding our military working dogs for their service," explains Aiello, the group simply asked for official sanction of the organization in issuing the United States Military Working Dog Service Award. You can guess the result.

Because he and his team knew how much it meant for handlers to have some recognition for their dogs, they went ahead and created the United States Military Working Dog Service Award anyway. It can be bestowed on any dog who has actively participated in ground or surface combat. It's a large bronze-colored medal on a red, white, and blue neck ribbon. It comes with a personalized certificate. There have been about eighty awarded so far, and Aiello says handlers greatly appreciate their dogs being recognized like this.

The move to see dogs get some kind of official recognition is gaining support from those inside, as well. In 2011, Master Chief Scott Thompson, head of military working dog operations in Afghanistan at the time, spoke at a biannual conference at Lackland Air Force Base. He said that these dogs absolutely deserve medals. "Some veterans may say it's degrading to them, but it shouldn't be. Most commanders have given dogs Purple Hearts, but it wouldn't have to be the same awards. I think most people would agree that dogs have earned the right to this. There needs to be some kind of legislation to recognize what dogs do, and we need to do the right thing."

There was once a German shepherd mix who received an official Distinguished Service Cross, a Purple Heart, and a Silver Star. His name was Chips. He performed many feats of courage and loyalty while serving in World War II, but one event in particular shows what this dog was made of. In the dark of early morning on July 10, 1943, on a beach in Sicily, Chips and his handler, Private John P. Rowell, came under machine-gun fire from a camouflaged pillbox. Here's how Michael Lemish describes it in his book *War Dogs*:

> *Immediately Chips broke loose from Rowell, trailing his leash and running full-steam toward the hut. Moments later, the machine-gun fire stopped and an Italian soldier appeared with Chips slashing and biting his arm and throat. Three soldiers followed with their arms raised in surrender. Rowell called Chips off and took the four Italians prisoner. What actually occurred in the pillbox is known only by the Italians, and, of course, the dog. Chips received a minor scalp wound and displayed powder burns, showing that a vicious fight had taken place inside the hut and that the soldiers had attempted to shoot the dog with a revolver. But the surrender came abruptly, indicating that Chips was solely responsible.*

That night, Chips also alerted to ten Italian soldiers moving in on them. Rowell was able to take them all prisoners because of his dog's warning. Chips was lauded for his heroism and highly decorated. But William Thomas, national commander of the Military Order of the Purple Heart, was not amused. "It decries the high and lofty purpose for which the medal was created." The War Department rescinded the dog's awards, and the medals were returned.

Major General J. A. Ulio would go on to decree the following year that "the award of War Department decorations to other than persons, that is, human beings, is prohibited." (You've got to love the clarification of "other than persons.") But he also wrote that "if it is desired to recognize the outstanding services of an animal . . . appropriate citation may be published in unit general orders."

The latter clause left the door open for an official medal or award specifically for war dogs.

It's been nearly seventy years.

So this is how it looks if you want your dog to have a Purple Heart these days:

Air Force Staff Sergeant Brent Olson received a Purple Heart and an Army Commendation Medal for what happened the day he and his dog Blek (whom we met earlier in Part Four) were involved in an explosion in Afghanistan. Blek received nothing. At a ceremony where Olson was awarded another medal, he wanted Blek to receive his due recognition. He leaned over and pinned his own Purple Heart to Blek's harness.

"Everybody was like, 'awwwww!'" remembers Olson, "but I wanted to make a statement. Dogs are soldiers, too. They give up their whole lives for this. Sure they do it for the play and the fun, but the reason doesn't matter. They work so hard and save so many lives. Not to be recognized officially is a slap in the face."

If not a medal—at least not just yet—how about a stamp? All kinds of stamps come out every year. Among the 2012 selection are several flag designs, the ubiquitous love designs, some weather vanes, and some good-looking stamps featuring baseball greats and film directors. The year before brought a stamp featuring Owney, a really cool postal service dog from the late 1800s.

Sounds like at some point, stamps honoring military working dogs would have been a natural. That's what Aiello thought. He and his organization have been at the stamp issue since 2000. The last petition he sent with his official request had ten thousand signatures.

Connie Totten-Oldham, manager of stamp development for the U.S. Postal Service, recently wrote him saying, "I certainly can understand your interest in such an important subject and your frustration over your long campaign without seeing an actual stamp." She said she appreciates the many letters and petitions he has submitted through the years and that, as always, the matter is under consideration.

She suggested Aiello look into a souvenir cancellation postmark or services that provide personalized postage—you know, the kind of stamps featuring someone's baby or favorite cat. Aiello is not going that route. "I'm not going to settle for anything less than a postage stamp featuring these very deserving dogs." In case the postal service wants to know what it's up against, Aiello was a Vietnam war-dog handler. He and his scout dog, Stormy, routinely led many troops safely through the jungle, successfully completing missions, regardless of obstacles. . . .

All this is not to say that military working dogs are not memorialized or honored beyond, say, their memorial ceremonies. In fact, there are several privately funded war-dog memorial statues around the United States. A national memorial, also privately funded, and to be on public land in the Washington, D.C., area, is in the works.

And Ingraham's dog Rex will be featured in a traveling exhibition of twenty-one bronze portrait busts of military members starting in 2013. Artist Michael Jernigan met Rex and Ingraham while in Iraq. "I fell in love with him when I saw him. He had to be part of this."

Of course, you could ask what good are medals and stamps and statues for dogs? Do they even care? And the answer would be that no, they probably don't grasp the significance. What's another thing around their neck or a framed certificate on a wall? A dog would probably rather just get a treat or a Kong or, better yet, a belly rub.

The honors we bestow on canine heroes are really more for those who love them and live by them, those who have been saved by them. And who can say? Maybe the benefits of this go down the leash to the dog.

★ ★ ★ 55 ★ ★ ★

WALKING POINT, ONCE AGAIN

There's one thing you can pretty much guarantee for military dogs and handlers while we're fighting wars like this one, where a dog's senses are so essential: When they come home—*if* they come home—they're going back to war, for as long as this war endures. "It's only a matter of time. It's not *if* they go back, but *when*," says Master Chief Thompson.

"If there's a fight, the handlers and dogs will be there leading the way, and they're going back, and the handlers know that." Thompson pauses, trying to keep his composure. "They go back, and they don't complain, and their dogs don't complain. And hopefully they get to go home again. . . ."

The Black Hawk gone, EOD tech Mesa ran back to his men and fired with them until the insurgents stopped shooting. They didn't bother looking to see if they'd hurt or killed any of them.

A marine bolted over to Fenji. She was still on the ground,

shaking. He stroked her and encouraged her to walk. She tried, and stumbled to the ground. So he picked her up. Her ears were bleeding from inside, and there was something wrong with her eyes.

A helicopter flew Fenji to Camp Leatherneck, a large Marine Corps base that's the hub for marine activity in Helmand Province. Her eardrums had been ruptured from the blast, and the explosion had rocketed debris into her eyes. You have to wonder if she was waiting for Donahue to come help her. In a way, he already had helped her. His body shielded her from the blast, so she was not seriously injured.

Fenji got top veterinary care, and attention from the marine handlers who came through the kennels. Gunnery Sergeant Chris Willingham, who was Donahue's kennel master back at Camp Pendleton, became a regular visitor. "We'd take Fenji for walks, spend time with her, flush out her eyes, take her to daily checkups. She was always glad for the company and had a good attitude. She was a real trouper," he says.

She attended a memorial for Donahue at Camp Leatherneck. Before it started, she went up to the front of the tent and stared at his photo, next to the normal memorial setup of combat boots and rifle. Those weren't his, but the dog tags and her leash hanging off the rifle were. You wonder if she could still smell his scent on them.

The kennels at Camp Leatherneck got a new name after this: Camp Donahue. At the entry point is a large concrete slab with a big ink rendition of Donahue and Fenji, created by a couple of guys in his platoon. Several marines built the structure that protects it, kind of a peaked-roof topper, with a large flagpole behind it.

Fenji gradually recovered, and three weeks after that terrible day, she flew back to Camp Pendleton. There she got more R & R and slowly started engaging in activities. They thought she'd probably retire, but as Willingham says, "She never lost her edge." Fenji received the Purple Heart and a Combat Action ribbon—unofficially of course.

It was three weeks before she was exposed to gunfire again. At first she cowered and flinched, so they took it easy on her. But she got used to it quickly. It probably helped that she was getting lots of love and attention from handlers and higher-ups during this time. "We'd groom her and let her come into the office and hang out with us," said Gunnery Sergeant Justin Green, who'd known Donahue for years. "It's what Max would have wanted, and she loved it."

I came upon Fenji at the predeployment course at the Yuma Proving Ground almost one full year to the date after she was injured. I had no idea what her background was, or what she had been through. I just saw a beautiful black shepherd wearing Doggles with camouflage frames. I'd been hoping to see a dog in Doggles during my travels, so I asked Gunny Knight about her, and he introduced me to Corporal Andrei Idriceanu, who had gone to Afghanistan with Donahue and subsequently helped care for Fenji.

We crouched under the shade of low, chunky palm trees, and I learned the main part of Fenji's story. As Idriceanu talked, Fenji kept rubbing her face against his leg. Such affection, I thought. But that wasn't it. She was trying to remove her Doggles. "She hates them, she's always trying to take them off," he said.

She was wearing them under doctor's orders. Idriceanu thought it was because of her eye injury, but Yuma veterinarian Emily Pier-acci says that although Fenji still has white spots in her right eye because of damage from the blast, they don't seem to affect her vision. The Doggles are for pannus, a common autoimmune dis-ease in German shepherds. It's made worse by ultraviolet light, thus the protective Doggles. Eventually the pannus will make Fenji blind. Medication and Doggles will slow the progression of the con-dition. She'll have frequent vision checks from now on to track her eyesight.

The big test at Yuma was to see how she reacted to gunfire and IED simulators. Would she cower or try to run off? Would she be brought back to one year ago, when the sounds rendered her deaf and nearly blind, and in great pain—and took her beloved han-dler? No. She did great. Never flinched or cowered, kept right on with her exercises. She performed like a champion soldier dog.

A couple of months after I met her, Fenji got on a C-17 and flew back to Afghanistan with her new handler for a seven-month rota-tion.

Once again walking point, with her handler close behind.

All interviews in this book were conducted between May and October 2011, either in person, by phone, or via e-mail. Rarely did I have e-mail contact only.

Interviews with several sources are used throughout the book—for background and/or direct quotation—and cannot be categorized neatly into one or two sections below. These wide-ranging sources are Air Force Master Sergeant Antonio "Arod" Rodriguez, Marine Gunnery Sergeant Kristopher Knight, "Doc" Stewart Hilliard, Air Force Major William Roberts, Marine Captain John "Brandon" Bowe, Michael Lemish, Air Force Technical Sergeant Joseph Null, Gerry Proctor, Nancy Ori (Department of Defense military working dog inventory manager), Brandon Liebert, and Navy Master Chief Scott Thompson.

In doing research for this book, I pored through hundreds of publications, including newspapers and magazine articles, government documents, Web site posts, scientific studies, PowerPoint presentations, and books. This research was primarily to bolster my background and knowledge of the topic. In this section I cite only publications I directly quote or refer to in the book.

PART ONE

"1st Cavalry Division, 7th Regiment, Hq. & Hq. Co., K-9 Platoon First K-9 Unit to See Combat During the Korean War," USWardogs.org, http://www.uswardogs.org/id89.html.

Harris, Gardiner. "A Bin Laden Hunter on Four Legs," *New York Times*, May 4, 2011, http://www.nytimes.com/2011/05/05/science/05dog.html.

Interviews with Marine Sergeant Rosendo Mesa, Marine Gunnery Sergeant Justin Green, Marine Gunnery Sergeant Chris Willingham, Marine Corporal Andrei Idriceanu, Julie Schrock, Navy Lieutenant Commander John Gay, Amanda Lothian, Ron Aiello, Victoria Stillwell, Army Sergeant Amanda Ingraham, Army Staff Sergeant Marcus Bates.

Johnson, Garth. "Awww: A War Dog Helped Take Out Osama," *Gothamist*, May 4, 2011, http://gothamist.com/2011/05/04/awww_a_war_dog_helped_take_out_osam.php.

Kriel, Robyn. "Civilian Casualties Helped by Marines in Safar Bazaar Garmsir Province Afghanistan," http://www.youtube.com/watch?v=uBIzVysaJXs&feature=mfu_in_order&list=UL.

Lemish, Michael G. *War Dogs: A History of Loyalty and Heroism* (Dulles, VA: Potomac Books, Inc., 2008).

Waller, Anna M. *Dogs and National Defense*, Department of the Army, Office of the Quartermaster General, 1958, http://www.qmmuseum.lee.army.mil/dogs_and_national_defense.htm.

PART TWO

"Funny Police Dog Fail," http://www.youtube.com/watch?v=jTDn0-jIm7k.

Interviews with Marine Lieutenant Colonel Kenneth Burger (program manager for the Improvised Explosive Device Detector Dog [IDD] capability), Navy Master-at-Arms First Class

McAuthor Parker, Navy Senior Chief Machinist Mate Sean Craycraft, Navy Master-at-Arms Third Class Cameron Frost, Ronnie Nye DVM, John Engstrom, John Bradshaw, David Garcia, Air Force Staff Sergeant Richard Crotty, Air Force Master Sergeant Richard Reidel (341st Training Squadron operations superintendent), Air Force Technical Sergeant Justin Marshall, Air Force Technical Sergeant Jason Barken, Navy Master-at-Arms First Class Ekali Brooks, Navy Master-at-Arms Seaman Glenn Patton, Victoria Stillwell, Mark Hines (Canine Behavior and Training Specialist, Kong Co.).

Richardson, Lieutenant Colonel Edwin H. *British War Dogs: Their Training and Psychology* (London: Skeffington & Son, Ltd., 1920).

Statement of Work: Potential Military Working Dogs, 341st Training Squadron, 2006, www.lackland.af.mil/shared/media/document/AFD-061211-005.pdf.

"Your Country Needs Your Dog," Mod.uk, http://www.mod.uk/DefenceInternet/AboutDefence/WhatWeDo/Trainingand Exercises/DefenceAnimalCentre/YourCountryNeedsYourDog .htm.

PART THREE

Bradshaw, John. *Dog Sense: How the New Science of Dog Behavior Can Make You a Better Friend to Your Pet* (New York: Basic Books, 2011).

Coren, Stanley. *How Dogs Think: What the World Looks Like to Them and Why They Act the Way They Do* (New York: Free Press, 2005).

Interviews with Alexandra Horowitz, Air Force Technical Sergeant Gwendolyn Dodd, Marine Staff Sergeant Kenny Porras, Marine Corporal Charles "Cody" Haliscak, Navy Master-at-Arms Second Class Joshua Raymond, Air Force Technical Sergeant Adam Miller, Army Captain Emily Pieracci DVM, John Bradshaw, Stanley Coren, Navy Lieutenant Commander John Gay, Marine Corporal Wesley Gerwin, Brian Hare, Alice and Duane Putnam, Jingzhi "Hippo" Tan.

Stillwell, Victoria. *Inside of a Dog: What Dogs See, Smell, and Know* (New York: Scribner, 2009).

PART FOUR

Dalton, Curt. "The Dog Days of War," DaytonHistoryBooks.com: http://www.daytonhistorybooks.com/page/page/1640971.htm.

Fimrite, Peter. "Marine, Dog to Reunite After Hard Journey for Both," *San Francisco Chronicle*, November 24, 2011.

"Guardians of the Night," K9Pride.com, http://k9pride.com/2008/05/06/guardians-of-the-night/.

Interviews with Marine Sergeant Mark Vierig, Air Force Staff Sergeant Brent Olson, Air Force Staff Sergeant Chris Keilman, Army Sergeant Amanda Ingraham, Robert Kollar, Walter Burghardt, DVM, Kelly Mann, DVM, Nicola J. Rooney (Research Fellow, University of Bristol Anthrozoology Institute), Marine Sergeant Rosendo Mesa, Julie Schrock, John Engstrom, Sylvana Stratton, James Bailey, Larry and Lynette Sargent, Debbie Kandoll, Jerry and Karen Self, Ron Aiello, Michael Jernigan, Marine Gunnery Sergeant Chris Willingham, Marine Gunnery Sergeant Justin Green, Marine Corporal Andrei Idriceanu.

Lemish, Michael G. *War Dogs: A History of Loyalty and Heroism* (Dulles, VA: Potomac Books Inc., 2008).

Letter from Connie Totten-Oldham, manager of stamp development for the U.S. Postal Service, to Ron Aiello, president, United States War Dog Association, September 19, 2011.

Letter to Sen. John Warner from William Putney, DVM, October 18, 2000, Congressional Record, V. 146, Pt. 16, October 13, 2000, to October 24, 2000.

McCombs, Phil. "A Soldier's Best Friend," *The Washington Post*, November 25, 2000.

The Papers of George Washington—Documents, October 6, 1777, http://gwpapers.virginia.edu/documents/revolution/howe .html.

Perry, Tony. "Afghanistan's Most Loyal Troops," *Los Angeles Times*, February 8, 2011.

"PFC Colton Wesley Rusk, USMC," http://www.sawyergeorge funeralhome.com/obituaries/2010/12/pfc-colton-wesley-rusk -usmc/.

Roughton, Randy. "Fallen Marine's Family Adopts His Best Friend," U.S. Department of Defense, February 4, 2011, http://www.defense.gov/news/newsarticle.aspx?id=62703.

Schrock, Julie Burget. *Missing Max: Finding Hope After My Marine Son's Death* (Altamonte Springs, FL: Advantage Inspirational, 2011).

★ ★ ★ ACKNOWLEDGMENTS ★ ★ ★

A platoon of dedicated men and women—both military and civilian—had my back throughout this book. I am really lucky to have had their support in telling the story of these devoted handlers and their incredible military working dogs.

Arod (Master Sergeant Antonio Rodriguez) was always a phone call or e-mail away, day or night, from the very beginning of this project. He may not have a starring role in the pages of this book, but he was there every step of the way, supplying me with credible sources, rich background information, and an honest look at every aspect of the military working dog world. His goal from the outset was just to get these handlers and dogs the recognition they richly deserve.

Gunny (Gunnery Sergeant Kristopher Knight) was also deeply devoted to helping tell the story of these teams. He provided me with invaluable contacts and behind-the-scenes info, and unprecedented access. And like Arod, he pulled no punches when it came to telling it like it is. The fact that neither of these guys is a sheeple has greatly benefited the book.

If it hadn't been for Gerry Proctor, the public affairs officer at Lackland Air Force Base, this book would have been left at the gates of a vital part of the Military Working Dog Program. He does not grant this kind of book-author access easily or lightly, and I am indebted to him for seeing that this was a project worth supporting.

Also to thank at Lackland for their hard work in regularly getting me the info I needed: "Doc" Stewart Hilliard, Air Force

Master Sergeant Richard Reidel, Nancy Ori, Ronnie Nye, DVM, and Walter Burghardt, DVM.

Air Force Staff Sergeant Andrew Rounds, Navy Master-at-Arms First Class McAuthor Parker, Navy Master-at-Arms Second Class Lisette La Torrre, Navy Master-at-Arms Seaman Silvia Cureses, and Navy Master-at-Arms Second Class David Gutierrez are among many who contributed excellent information and stories that did not make it into the book in the final cut because of space constraints.

Lieutenant Commander John Gay, public affairs officer at Navy Expeditionary Combat Command in Virginia, worked overtime to get me access to a submarine with a jaunty little dog inspecting it for bombs. I'm grateful to him for letting me see the many ways the navy uses dogs and for his introduction to Master Chief Scott Thompson, who had just gotten back from his yearlong command of the dog program in Afghanistan.

I'm deeply grateful to Julie Schrock, Corporal Max Donahue's mother, for being able to open up and talk about her son, which, if painful for me, must have been almost unbearable for her at times. And to all the marines who helped fill me in on Donahue's story.

A salute to Marine Captain John "Brandon" Bowe for his across-the-board support, and to Bill Childress, Marine Military Working Dog Program manager.

Michael Lemish generously assisted me in delving into this history of military dogs, and Ron Aiello helped me look to both the past and future of these dogs.

In the realm of the senses and sciences, a big thanks to John Bradshaw, Alexandra Horowitz, and Stanley Coren for their contributions. Hats off to Korrina Duffy, at the Duke Canine Cognition Center, and to Brian Hare, who heads the center with aplomb.

ACKNOWLEDGMENTS

There are several people I'm grateful for on the editorial side of things: Agent Deirdre Mullane, for seeking me out to do this book after finding out about my passion for military working dogs, and for helping me whip the proposal into shape in record time; agent Carol Mann, for her usual great work throughout; Dutton editor Stephen Morrow, for his enthusiasm for the book and his superb guidance and suggestions; Dutton's Stephanie Hitchcock, for dotting the i's and crossing the t's; writer Mark MacNamara, for his eye for a good story; clearance consultant Valarie Barsky, for her fine work in getting all permissions and clearances in order; Kimball Worcester, because how often does a copy editor specializing in military history move in next door the day you sign a military book contract?; Janine Kahn, for holding down the fort at Dogster while I took a leave of absence to finish this book; author Jane Miller, for helping Deirdre Mullane find me; and writer Daniela Caride, of Taildom, for bending over backward to share her sources when I was fresh out the gate.

A heartfelt *grazie* to my terrific husband, Craig Hanson, for pitching in with everything during the extremely busy months of putting this book together, and ditto to our daughter, Laura, for hanging in there and being a great kid while I disappeared into this book.

Finally, to all the military working dog handlers who let me into their lives, and to their dogs: You have gained my utmost respect and admiration.